D0143602

of related interest

Anorexics on Anorexia
Edited by Rosemary Shelley
ISBN 978 1 85302 471 9

Beating Eating Disorders Step by Step
A Self-Help Guide for Recovery
Anna Paterson
ISBN 978 1 84310 340 0

Inside Anorexia
The Experiences of Girls and their Families
Christine Halse, Anne Honey and Desiree Boughtwood
IBN 978 1 84310 597 8

Bulimics
on Bulimia

Edited by Maria Stavrou

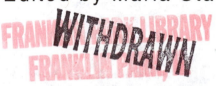

Jessica Kingsley Publishers
London and Philadelphia

First published in 2009
by Jessica Kingsley Publishers
116 Pentonville Road
London N1 9JB, UK
and
400 Market Street, Suite 400
Philadelphia, PA 19106, USA

www.jkp.com

Copyright © Jessica Kingsley Publishers 2009

Library of Congress Cataloging in Publication Data

Bulimics on bulimia / Edited by Maria Stavrou.
   p. cm.
  ISBN 978-1-84310-668-5 (pb : alk. paper)
  1. Bulimia. I. Stavrou, Maria.
  RC552.B84B865 2009
  616.85'263--dc22

                           2008015158

British Library Cataloguing in Publication Data
A CIP catalogue record for this book is available from the British Library

ISBN 978 1 84310 668 5

Printed and bound in the United States by
Thomson-Shore, 7300 Joy Road, Dexter, MI 48130

Contents

Acknowledgements

Karen Ciclitira for her support and guidance in my final year research project on bulimia.

The contributors for their courage in sharing their experiences.

Panayis and Christina Stavrou. Kyriakos, Androulla, Evangelia and Andreas Ttofi. Katina, Marios, Liza, Kyriaki and Nadia Christodoulou.

Samantha Pottinger, Victoria Spicer, Siobhan Howse, Gemma, Katie, Kader, Derya Irfan, Semele Meade, Zoe Robinson, Rina Kashmiri, Charlene Goodman, Yasemin, Camilla Phillips, Adele Phillips, Paris Ray, Biana Louise Hammond, Nancy Allotey and Hatice Ali. Sunbul Akhter, Paulette Barrish and Madiha Chaudry.

Georgina Charalambides, Daniela Parente, Maria Lambrou, Lisa Gammalliere, Louise Warren and Laura Stephens.

Introduction

The aim of this book is to provide a sample of insights into what life is like *living with* bulimia. The vast majority of books currently published do not provide such an accurate reflection of everyday life with bulimia. Many books on the disorder are written while the writers are in recovery, as a retrospective account of bulimia. This book tries to capture an accurate reflection of life with bulimia, with women in all stages of the disorder, either actively engaged in bulimic behaviors or recovering/recovered. Retrospective accounts are valuable and provide insight into the disorder, but there is a problem with them in that they cannot be as accurate. Someone who still struggles with this disorder will believe "I need this to cope and it's all that I have."

Bulimia affects an increasing number of people. It is a silent, secretive disorder, more common than most people realize. It is not just a problem of young girls in schools or college campuses; it affects a much wider range of people. Bulimia is often seen, particularly by medical professionals, as the "lesser" disorder to anorexia nervosa. Bulimia's reputation as the "lesser" disorder to anorexia is gravely misguided. Coverage of anorexia seems to dominate the media and medical journals but bulimia is largely ignored or trivialized. This is not surprising considering that bulimia is a much easier disorder to hide than anorexia. There is also the issue with diagnostic labeling. A considerable amount of people diagnosed with anorexia are not abstaining from food but are engaging in bulimic behaviors who would, with the exception of their weight, meet every diagnostic criteria for bulimia. To elaborate, an overweight or average weight individual who binges and purges can be diagnosed with bulimia. However, if this person loses weight to be medically classified as underweight, they will be given a new diagnosis of anorexia with purging subtype. This diagnosis would mean that an underweight individual is regarded as "anorexic" with its stigma of "nervous loss of appetite", despite eating large amounts of food every day. This can be a semi-inaccurate label or it could potentially be damaging to research on bulimia. The labeling system of eating disordered patients can, therefore, distort the research and statistical findings into bulimia. It can also cause patients to lose trust in the medical and psychiatric profession.

As an example of this loss of trust, in speaking to individuals with bulimia regarding what they knew of research of the disorder, they thought of an example of a study conducted that measured the amount of food eaten and the proportion of the food that was vomited back up. It was found that only a small percentage of the food eaten is vomited and most of the food is digested and it is concluded by medical professionals that bulimia is not an effective method of getting rid of the calories from the food and so therefore not an effective method of weight loss. First, if the study included individuals who have been labeled as "anorexic with purging subtype" but still binge and purge perhaps even every day and multiple times a day, the findings of the study would be more accurate. Second, when medical professionals tell their patients with bulimia that it is not an effective weight loss method and the patients have seen for themselves that it is, they lose trust and will also lose trust in anything else the medical professional has to say, including accurate and important information on health issues and concerns. It has even been suggested to patients by their doctors that they must simply be lying or over-exaggerating the extent to which they are eating, the frequency of the binges and that the food they eat must not qualify as a binge at all. I know many women either underweight, average weight or overweight who binge and purge. These women could binge and purge a couple of times a week (the minimum in a week for a period of at least nine months so a diagnosis of bulimia is made), several times a week, once a day or several times a day. Bulimia can be quite accurately described as one of the most insidious mental disorders, largely unseen but with potentially fatal consequences.

The health risks associated with bulimia include swollen salivary glands (commonly understood by the term "chipmunk cheeks"), digestive disorders such as heartburn, indigestion, bloating and reflux, diminished mental capacity (less ability to concentrate), a weaker immune system (increasing the susceptibility to colds and bugs), electrolyte imbalances that are essential for the heart to function, causing palpitations (purging and especially use of laxatives can deplete these essential minerals and put the heart at risk) and an increased likelihood of developing depression, anxiety disorders or addiction to substances such as alcohol or drugs.

This book has been inspired by Rosemary Shelley, editor of *Anorexics on Anorexia* (1997). After reading *Anorexics on Anorexia* I eagerly waited for the publication of another similar book and to the prospect of reading the stories from the point of view of people with bulimia. After many years of no such book, I decided to attempt compiling such a book myself. I feel it is important that the struggle many individuals face with bulimia is published as there is much misinformation and confusion on bulimia. Some of the many myths I have heard on the disorder are that only teenage girls suffer from it, it is not a serious disorder as anorexia is and you cannot die from bulimia. I had even read in an old psychology textbook during my years studying psychology for an undergraduate degree that only women and gay men suffer from bulimia. This is not true as many men also suffer regardless of their sexuality, although it is less common among men compared to women. Unfortunately and regrettably, the male perspective on this disorder is not represented as no men came forward to share their experiences.

As expected, there are common themes coming up throughout the contributors' stories. Binge eating most often occurs after a bout of restricting dietary intake. Restricting food intake could refer to dieting or to anorexia nervosa. Restricting leads to extreme hunger, or starvation mode, and cravings for high calorie foods. Obsessive thoughts about food and weight are magnified by restriction. Dieting and anorexic behaviors are addictive and it is not unheard of for women with bulimia to feel like "failed anorexics" or to desire the ability to restrict dietary intake and feel "in control":

> I longed for restriction. I missed the days when I could easily control what I ate. I missed being able to survive on minimal food. I still craved feeling completely empty, only now I could only achieve that through purging. Anorexia was definitely its own nightmare. I got to a dangerously low weight of 62 pounds while anorexic. I was constantly tired, weak and hungry. I was left almost completely isolated from the outside world. (Becca)

There are many examples throughout the book of the extreme restriction that the girls were, or still are, subjecting themselves to:

> Soon, I was purging every time alcohol hit my lips and because I was 18 and independent, alcohol would hit my lips at least three times a week. I quickly realized that if I could purge alcohol so easily, maybe I could purge the very little food I was eating. (Leah)

In many cases, women with bulimia restrict their intake when they are not binging and purging. There is a cyclic pattern to bulimia, the dieting leads to binge eating or over-eating, leads to guilt and then overcompensation and dieting again, which increases hunger and leads to overeating again and so on. A history of dieting is a common behavior before bulimic symptoms start:

> This is when I started to "diet." Dieting, to me, basically meant no desserts or snacks. Every Sunday morning, I would start a new diet. I would have a small bowl of cereal (never sugary stuff) and a small glass of juice. Naturally, by the time lunch rolled around, five hours later, I was famished. So I would generally screw up the "diet" and have to start again the next day. I never lost any weight doing this, but I kept trying. (Marilyn)

The idea to self-induce vomiting is usually brought on by the sudden guilt of going off the planned restrictive food intake. In one case, the food intake was 500 calories:

I would eat only 500 calories a day to do so. This went on for quite some time, but a body can only tolerate such a diet for so long. Thus, I discovered purging. If I ever went over 500 calories, up the food came. (Bethany)

Individuals with bulimia will go to great lengths to hide their disorder from family and friends. This guilt and desire to keep bulimic behaviors hidden from family and friends is unrelenting. The purging eases the guilt:

I had just done what I never would have done before. But it was okay because I could get rid of it. Erase the guilt and go on as if it never even happened. I was going to be okay. Or so I thought. (Becca)

The bulimic behavior is justified as a normal, necessary and routine part of life:

Food was a central part of the family. It represented love and what the family used to share their affection for each other. Physical fullness and hunger really had little, or anything, to do with what you did or did not eat. The better food was reserved for those who deserved it and you ate what was given to you, pretty much as an acceptance of the giver's love. If you didn't want to eat then you needed a reason and a real, deal, solid reason. Saying you just ate was often seen as an excuse but also brought on intense guilt when the interaction would become, "Well just sit down... have a little... for me..." In those moments the debate in my head was usually whose feelings are first. (Domna)

There is a strong association that is made and passed on to children that it is bad to "eat too much" or to eat the "wrong" types of food. The guilt is connected to the food from such an early age it is intricately linked, it becomes ingrained, an assumption, a negative and damaging core belief:

> I would sneak into the kitchen when everyone else was busy, grab cookies or bread or whatever I could get quickly and quietly, stuff it into my pockets and run upstairs to eat it before anyone saw me. If I were to get caught, I would be in trouble. (Marilyn)

This guilt and struggle with food can increase feelings of low self-esteem. Self-worth is judged by the numbers on the scale, the ability to restrict well in between binging and purging episodes, the ability to purge the food effectively so as not to gain weight, the ability to hide these behaviors from family and friends and maintain an outward appearance of calm and normality. It is a fine balance and can, in part, add to the mood swings common with bulimia. There is a constant need and struggle to control these behaviors and to maintain everything "just right." Anything other than "just right" can result in extreme thinking, where suddenly "everything is going wrong", "I'm useless… a failure… worthless."

> I had already lost most of my self-esteem, personality and ambition to succeed in any part of life that didn't involve calories, weight or food. What else did I really have left to lose? Apparently, oh so very much more. (Sara)

> I took everything personally and every mistake or correction was interpreted as a personal failure, proof that I was hopeless and would never be good enough. I wanted to be good enough. I wanted my parents' approval. I wanted them to be proud of me. I could never get this from them, my personality was not what they wanted. (Marilyn)

> I am still not good enough. My house is not clean enough, my grades aren't high enough, my son isn't obedient enough. I am not thin enough. I am obviously not good enough for my husband, if I were, then he wouldn't cheat on me. (Marilyn)

Bulimia can very quickly become an addiction. Life begins to revolve around what food you can get, where you can eat in secret and where you can purge without anyone hearing you. Or if you're not a purging bulimic, it will be how long you can go without eating to compensate for the binge, how many calories of the binge you can burn off by exercising or how many laxatives you'll take and hoping that they'll have their effect before you go to work or to school. Eating disorders have been compared to such addictions as smoking, alcoholism and drug addiction in the level of intensity. It has also been described of addictions that someone can live without and be teetotal from cigarettes, alcohol and drugs but not from food. Everyday brings decisions of what food is safe to eat so that it won't trigger a binge, when to stop eating, when to start, where you can eat that won't trigger a binge; as in front of the television is generally not good or anywhere else that you associate with binging (which may very well be everywhere). All these decisions are in addition to suppressing the nagging, gnawing urge that comes in mountainous waves. This urge is of needing to consume everything, push it right down (supposedly with the suppressed feelings and emotions), to fill yourself up, take the edge off the emptiness inside and then to violently empty yourself out, getting rid of the unwanted, you didn't need it anyway. The urge is to experience the blanket of security that is the post-purge high or the soothing, numbing calm of the release, assuring yourself that you are in control again, the intense feeling of relief.

Due to the cyclic nature of bulimia, the dieting, guilt and overeating, it is not surprising there is a strong addictive nature to bulimia. I believe this addiction is not just a result of the restriction and the guilt, although they do greatly enhance it. The addiction is far deeper; it is physical, psychological and can become a deeply entrenched habit, as hard to break as a heroin addiction:

> Bulimia is my addiction. I binge and purge because I feel an irreconcilable urge to do so… Life now revolved around food, reading about it, looking at it, finding it, buying it and binging and purging on it. I started rearranging my life to accommodate my obsession… I became obsessed with food. When I wasn't buying or binging on food I was reading about it, looking at pictures of it, dreaming about it… I decided I needed to start weighing myself before binging and after purging in order to ensure I was emptying completely. I discovered the phenomenon of "rinsing" which is really just a term for drinking glasses of water and then purging over and over again until "rinsing clear"… Bulimia now feels like the only way I know how *not* to kill myself. Now I feel like I'm binging and purging to stay alive. Sometimes the urge is so strong I feel like I'll literally collapse and die if I don't act on it. (Becca)

> Bulimia is my safety net and my destruction. I don't know if I can survive in this world without having my crutch and I don't know how much longer I can survive in this world with my crutch because it is slowly killing me. (Sara)

As well as these commonalities, the contributors in this book also face individual struggles and experiences, possibly even reinforcing their bulimic behaviors: type-one juvenile diabetes, sexual abuse, bankruptcy, destructive friendships, being a performing artist, culture, working for the Unites States air force, alcoholism (another coping mechanism) and self-harm (another relatively common coping mechanism among bulimics):

> Binging and purging and self-harming have become my most frequently used "solutions" to problems. I turn to them when I'm stressed, angry, sad or anxious. They are very flawed

coping mechanisms in that their effects are usually very short-lived. (Becca)

At 15, I started cutting myself as a way to take the edge off. Cutting numbed me. Self-harm calmed my raging emotions and somehow made everything seem okay. (Marilyn)

My world began to slowly crumble even in high school as depression began to creep into my life with bouts of self-harm. My college years were interrupted with suicide attempts and self-harm that was so serious I was going to the emergency room every week. (Bethany)

Hospitals can recommend certain self-help books in order to aid the process of recovery for their patients. The self-help books recommended to overcome binge eating and purging are *Getting Better Bit(e) by Bit(e)* by the Eating Disorder Clinic in the Maudsley Hospital, London and *Overcoming Binge Eating* is recommended in the Phoenix Wing of St. Ann's Hospital, London.

1

Binging and Purging to Stay Alive

I hear it so often, "I could never be bulimic. I hate throwing up." Yeah? Me too. I laugh every time because it implies I must have started purging because I have some weird fondness for throwing up. That's not true. I don't like it, but that is practically irrelevant at this point. Bulimia is my addiction. I binge and purge because I feel an irreconcilable urge to do so. I never planned on making this my life, it just kind of turned out that way.

I spent the first six years of my eating disorder trying to convince myself I hated food. I considered it a sign of weakness to admit I was hungry or that I had any desire to eat. During those six years I secretly longed for the ability to make myself throw up. It is a sick thing to wish for but not entirely crazy when I considered what I thought to be the only alternative, depriving myself of any food I deemed "bad." If only I could purge, I could eat all the things I so rarely was able to enjoy. To the casual outsider, that is what bulimia is, "eating whatever you want and then throwing up." It is only those who have experienced both its glory and its horror who know it is actually much more than that.

I quickly caught on to the mechanics of successful purging and in the beginning, it was great. I started trying things I was always too afraid to try before. Food was fun again. I still remember the first time I ate an entire box of chocolate chip cookies. I stared in amazement at the empty box for a good five minutes. I was both horrified and fascinated all at once. I had just done what I never would have done before. But it was okay because I could get rid of it. Erase the guilt and go on as if it never even happened. I was going to be okay. Or so I thought.

Bulimia quickly took control of my life. School, friends and anything that once meant something to me were now secondary to this new activity. Life now revolved around food, reading about it, looking at it, finding it, buying it and binging and purging on it. I started rearranging my life to accommodate my obsession. Classes were no longer a priority. I went when I could tolerate sitting still for more than an hour. Homework and papers were something I did while waiting for food to cook and in between binge and purge sessions. I was late for everything. I always thought I could fit in just one more binge and purge before I left. I learned to be fairly quick when I needed to be, but usually not quick enough. Three-hour night classes were a nightmare. I tried to binge and purge quickly on the ten-minute break they gave us but almost always lost track of time. I got tired of walking into class late so I just stopped going.

The library was no longer a place to study but a place to purge when I felt too ashamed to purge in the dorm bathrooms again. I made at least two trips a day to the grocery store to stock up on more food. I quickly learned to vary the places I went so as not to look too suspicious. At first I tried to hide it all from my roommates. I didn't want to binge in front of them so I was constantly stuffing my backpack full of food and carrying it around campus searching for new places to binge and purge in private. When people asked me why my bag was always so full I told them it was full of books and I was on my way to the library. They believed it for a while.

Soon it became too much to hide and I decided I didn't care anymore who saw me binging. I openly binged in my room in front of my roommate. I stayed up all night on my computer, getting up sometimes eight or nine times to purge. She knew what I was doing but didn't know what to say. It was soon so common it was not awkward at all. We even joked about it. She saw me coming in with armloads of groceries and knew it was going to be a busy night.

I was constantly exhausted and tired but there was no time to sleep. I thought every binge and purge would be the last one of the night but it never was. I started to judge the quality of my purging by how dizzy and shaky I felt afterwards. If I felt fine I must not have purged everything. I would eat something to keep from fainting, but nine times out of ten this just led to another binge and purge session. The cycle repeated itself until I was literally too tired to stay awake. Sleep was the only welcome interruption.

I quickly started losing contact with friends. I made excuses as to why I couldn't go out when really I was just too afraid to be away from the one thing I had come to both crave and despise. When I did go out I felt unbearably anxious and uncomfortable and couldn't wait to get back to the familiarity of binging and purging. At the end of my junior year my roommate and once best friend decided to stop talking to me. She told me she couldn't live with me anymore. The same girl who watched it all happen and laughed about it with me was now leaving. I hated her for it but at the same time understood and wondered why she didn't do it sooner.

The things that would have once repulsed me no longer did. I refused to start shoplifting food like so many bulimics do, so I had to learn to be creative about finding cheap or free food. I never turned down food offers. I used to take advantage of campus events where I knew food would be provided. Food left lying around or even in the trash suddenly didn't look so bad.

I was always hungry because I didn't allow myself to keep much down without purging. Eating a normal meal was too complicated. Somehow, binging and purging all day became easier than eating breakfast, lunch or dinner. Why drive myself insane trying to find something to eat that I won't feel guilty about when I could just eat whatever I wanted and then purge? I became obsessed with food. When I wasn't buying or binging on food I was reading about it, looking at pictures of it, dreaming about it. My idea of normal was extremely skewed. I knew this and yet I couldn't seem to think any other way.

I longed for restriction. I missed the days when I could easily control what I ate. I missed being able to survive on minimal food. I still craved feeling completely empty, only now I could only achieve that through purging. Anorexia was definitely its own nightmare. I got to a dangerously low weight of 62 pounds while anorexic. I was constantly tired, weak and hungry. I was left almost completely isolated from the outside world. Despite all of this, I still found bulimia more debilitating. Anorexia was clean, quiet and simple. Bulimia was messy, loud and complicated. I used to be neat and organized in everything I did. I had the perfect bedroom, the perfect grades and a seemingly perfect life. Bulimia left no room for organization. I dreaded the post binge and purge clean-up because I knew things would never stay clean for long. I filled up two large garbage bags every night. The carpet around and under my desk was ruined with food stains and my computer had been spilled on so many times there were several keys missing. I had to be careful not to get puke on my shoes. "Aim straight to avoid splashback," I told myself.

Everything would be done "right after this purge." A lot of people describe experiencing a "high" right after purging. For me the high was usually right after the binge and before the purge. I had this idea of the purge being the end of the madness and thus once it was over, all would be well. It was almost a manic feeling right after a particularly out of control binge. I felt larger than life, like I could accomplish anything just as soon as I purged. The purging would cleanse and empty me in such a way that I'd feel renewed and full of potential. I'd finally be able to write that paper, clean my room, whatever. I felt awful now, but all would be well just as soon as I purged. I continued to think this way even after learning otherwise. Everything would not get done "right after this purge" because "right after this purge" I usually felt even more miserable.

There is a common misconception that the act of purging is very straightforward. The movies make it look so simple. A girl eats an entire pizza, feels guilty and then goes to bathroom and gets sick. All this takes place in a matter of minutes. Sometimes it was that simple, but most of the time it was much more laborious. I quickly learned a simple heave or two wasn't going to cut it in terms of getting everything out. I was going to have to be more careful if I wanted to keep from gaining weight. I decided I needed to start weighing myself before binging and after purging in order to ensure I was emptying completely. I discovered the phenomenon of "rinsing" which is really just a term for drinking glasses of water and then purging over and over again until "rinsing clear." This is when I knew I was getting everything up, or as much as I possibly could. Sometimes though, the scale refused to budge. When this happened, I would panic. How could there possibly still be stuff inside me when I just spent the past 45 minutes purging? I started feeling unaccomplished until I was throwing up blood on a regular basis.

Today most of my friends are the people I met in hospitals or treatment centers. My best friend is also bulimic. I worry about her every day. It hurts me that she is in such pain. It's not fair. She deserves to be happy and healthy. I want her to like herself. I want her to see what everyone else sees when we look at her. I'm mad she has to go through it at all and I'm upset I can't seem to do much to make it better. Her being self-destructive is not okay. I don't know why I hold myself to such a different standard.

If this life is making me so miserable, why do I continue to live this way? Most people don't understand that eating disorders are about a lot more than food or wanting to be thin. There are hundreds of reasons why people develop eating disorders or why they continue to deal with them for so long. It can take years of therapy to uncover all of the reasons. Often, eating disorder symptoms are used to cope with difficult events and situations. Binging and purging and self-harming have become my most frequently used "solutions" to problems. I turn to them when I'm stressed, angry, sad or anxious. They are very flawed coping mechanisms in that their effects are usually very short-lived. In treatment I have learned all about alternative coping skills, but somehow being self-destructive still seems like the most available option. I usually crave immediate as opposed to long-term gratification, making the symptoms seem worth all of their accompanying side effects.

There are also those times when I felt like I was passively trying to kill myself by staying in my disorder. There have been periods in my life when I felt so defeated and hopeless that I was pretty certain I wanted to die. I was using the bulimia as a slow way to bring about my death. I no longer see my eating disorder in this way. Bulimia now feels like the only way I know how *not* to kill myself. Now I feel like I'm binging and purging to stay alive. Sometimes the urge is so strong I feel like I'll literally collapse and die if I don't act on it. It makes no sense, but this has never been and never will be a logical illness.

There is ambivalence in recovery from any eating disorder or addiction. It is not as simple as just wanting to get better. Getting better comes with a whole slew of responsibilities and unknowns that often seem more daunting than staying sick. I am stuck. I am stuck between wanting to get out of this terrible place and clinging on to something I'm not sure I know how to live without.

2

There Goes Alice
Down the Hole

I still remember the day I first became bulimic. It was 1992 and I was just 11, in the fifth grade. I don't remember in my life ever not being weird about food, or even being horrified of becoming fat. Then one day I guess you could say curiosity got the best of me. I'd learned about bulimia and thought it seemed like it could work. So I excused myself from class one day after lunch, walked to the bathroom, pulled back my long wavy blonde hair and proceeded to stick two fingers down my throat until I'd successfully thrown up lunch. The most fitting way I know of describing what would follow is a lyric from a child's rhyme: "Oh my goodness, oh my soul, there goes Alice down the hole."

To this day I'm not sure what exactly caused me to even want to go down that road. I think it was more a variety of things. I have always wanted to be the best in every way, to achieve an almost unrealistic level of perfection. I also have always been sort of a loner. I like to be alone and do my own thing, yet at the same time I get incredibly, uncomfortably lonely. An eating disorder became almost like a friend.

As long as I have it, I don't need anyone else. Only, this too will eventually bite you in the ass. It's been years now since I first got curious. Yet here I am, wanting very much to be free of this, but still very much at times finding myself stuck. I jumped down the hole and have fallen, stopping occasionally for a bit, sometimes even climbing a way back up, only to fall again, each time falling a bit further than the last. It's not at all that I don't want to be healthy, I do. It's just, bulimia, it seems is just as addictive as, say, smoking. Bulimia, also serves to fill a void in my life. Strange as it may seem, I've always had this sort of "something is missing" type of feeling. Two things thus far have ever served to fill that void – having an eating disorder and love.

I always thought I was invincible. I managed to keep things hidden for years. I'd always been thin as a child, so I think everyone just assumed it was natural. I'd also always been an incredibly picky eater, so it's understandable why when I started removing foods from my diet, it didn't seem like a big deal. For years I'd vacillated through periods of restriction, binging/purging and even rare occasional times of normalcy. I managed to get through most of junior high and high school without anyone noticing a thing.

After that first time in 1992, it would actually be nearly two years before I ever purposely puked again. Yet it was always a comforting feeling to know I could. By the sixth grade I just simply stopped eating anything but dinner. It's scary almost how easy it was to get away with. Breakfast I convinced myself made me nauseous, lunch many days just didn't get bought, or got thrown out. I was an unhappy child that year. I was the smart kid in class and everyone hated me for that. It seemed weight and food was the one thing I could control.

Only sometime in the next year I'd lose control. I don't remember when it started, I just remember suddenly realizing that I was eating again. This horrified me, so the only thing I could think to do was to start throwing up. I've often wondered if my best friend at the time wasn't doing the same. We'd eat boxes of pizza bagel bites at a time, as in bulk sized boxes. Yet, neither one of us ever seemed to gain an ounce from it. Looking back I think our friendship was almost as unhealthy as my being bulimic.

For the rest of junior high and high school I continued on this pattern. Starve, eat, freak, puke. Come senior year though, things got really bad. I'd moved with my parents and sister from a small town in southwest Michigan to a Detroit suburb in my junior year. It was never really that life there was so awful. In fact, there are things I still love about the area. Life at home, however, was anything but pleasant. It was literally out of control. I think my mother still blames my sister and me for that. By fall of senior year I was eating and throwing up every day, sometimes thousands of calories at a time. I worked overtime every week. Some days I'd even go into work and just sit in the back and chat with the boss. I think she suspected something was awry. Most nights I hardly slept at all. I'd run every night on the tread-mill, sometimes for hours, always hoping nobody would hear and wake up. Either they never did, or they just never said anything. I'd even gone from being a mostly A student to getting Bs and even occasional Cs because I spent far too much time skipping classes to throw up. I was going through bottles of diet pills much faster than anyone ever should. I was a wreck. Home life was out of control, nobody was happy and I just remember thinking this was the one thing I had control of. Eventually my parents and I decided I'd move back home and finish school. I think my mother still hates me for this. To her, any time I leave home it's like I don't want to be around her. That's unhealthy of her to think and incredibly untrue.

At some point that winter I stopped with the huge binges. I also, though, stopped eating much of anything at all. I'd have a fat-free yogurt and an oat-based cereal (no milk) for lunch, sometimes a granola bar and half a turkey sandwich or something else equally small. I never ate breakfast and rarely ate dinner. Yet, I always did the grocery shopping. I think I was obsessed with it even. By spring I'd lost enough weight that people started to notice and become concerned. Friends got angry with me, teachers started asking about it. I was fine though, I didn't need help. Even I started to wonder if I'd gone too far. I went out and bought myself a scale. I hadn't been on one in months and thought I'd use it to be sure I didn't really go overboard. Instead I became obsessed with watching the numbers go down.

I stayed home that next year and went to community college. Then in 2001 I transferred and moved to Colorado State University. I'd never been so far from home before, but in the end I still believe it was the best thing for me. For the first time in all those years, I actually went and got help. Also that year, when I went home, for the first time ever my parents decided to become openly concerned. Maybe they really do believe that I was fine all that time at home? Maybe it's just hard to see when it's right in front of you? I just remember feeling angry because for the first time I was trying to get better and suddenly I was being told I was worse. I started to question myself.

I'm not saying I didn't struggle, I did. I spent way too much time at the recreation center working out, became addicted to caffeine pills, mostly because I never had time to sleep. Yet, I had structure living on campus and that was at times helpful. It also helped that I had a Resident Assistant who caught on almost immediately and did a great job of intervening when things got questionable. She is now one of my good friends and I still thank God for putting her in my life. For the first time in the two years I lived on campus, I actually wanted to recover. Only that never completely happened.

Third year I moved off campus. Looking back, this was probably a mistake. Suddenly I felt alone and out of control. I started eating less, purging more and obsessively exercising again. I was literally starving. Then I went to my parents for spring break. They were in Florida, so I had the house to myself. I still remember that night. I decided to eat a graham cracker, just one, then two, three, four, the whole box, went back to the cupboard, macaroni and cheese, ravioli, cereal, an entire can of frosting, cake mix, to the fridge, milk, ice cream, cheese. I just kept going and going, eat, run to the bathroom, puke, do it all again. Right up until within just a few hours of being home, I'd managed to eat everything in the house. That's when things got really bad again. After that, I binged and purged literally every day from then on. I never ate a thing without puking any more. Then it happened, for the first time in all those years, June 2004, my eating disorder wound me up in the emergency room. So just one semester short of college graduation, I'd wind up on medical leave.

Time off school didn't automatically save me. In fact, at first and for about a year I got continually worse. I continued to purge everything I was eating the rest of that summer. That fall my parents moved to Indiana and I stayed at the house alone. Eventually I stopped sleeping at night. I would take sleeping pills and still just sit awake for days at a time. Most nights I spent exercising for hours on end or binging and purging, or both. Soon enough I would go days at a time without even eating, then go on these huge binge/purge fests. I was in therapy and in group, but it didn't seem to be helping. Then I suddenly one day pulled my act together enough to get a job. I guess I realized maybe I'd be a bit better off if I had something to do with at least some of my time.

Sometime that winter I moved in with a friend and his family. They knew about my struggles. They had family meals together all the time, which was uncomfortable at first but I got used to it. Granted, I was still going to work and purging every day. I would stop at gas stations on the way to appointments. I even was purging in doctors' offices. While the structure was good in some ways, by that time it wasn't enough to save me. That spring I wound up with bronchitis, totally unrelated but I did lose a few pounds. After that everything went way downhill again.

I was supposed to return to school the following fall. However, things got so bad again that my doctor at the time said absolutely not. I spent quite a few nights over the summer in the emergency room. After so long your body just starts to shut down, it's tired from all the abuse and things stop working right. My electrolyte levels would drop with no warning, sometimes even without cause. I'd be fine then get hit with sudden irregular heartbeats and chest pain. It was not a fun time. In August instead of going back to school, I wound up moving into a house with some girls from work. Just before that, I spent three days on a medical floor due to a dangerously low sodium level, which was causing me to pass out frequently, among other things. The unfortunate thing about eating disorders and medical care is that insurance basically sucks. It's hard to get them to cover it at all and a lot of times if you do wind up hospitalized as soon as your labs return stable they stop paying and you are sent home. Yet it's so easy to go from stable to not, even if you are actually eating right.

Living in my new house was not that great an idea either. One of the other girls was bulimic and the rest of our roommates would get annoyed at both of us for it. We had fun at times too though, maybe even too much. Yet once again I was eating nothing, purging what I did eat and literally falling apart. I was too sick to work most days. Then one night my friend came over because I was sick, the flu, I think I told her. Somehow she convinced me to go with her to the hospital. I don't know why I agreed, I was probably too tired or delirious to fight it. I spent the night in the emergency room on an intravenous drip trying to talk them into letting me leave. I knew at the back of my mind that I would be doing no such thing. I'm a social work major after all, so I know how this stuff works. Sure enough come morning the hospital social worker shows up with a bunch of paperwork. Either I sign myself in willingly and get to stay here at this nice place, or if I leave the hospital today they will call the police and I will end up somewhere likely not that nice.

Legally I had to stay for 72 hours. In this particular program, they tried to keep you until they felt you were ready and stable enough to leave. I was told I'd be there at least three weeks. However, because insurance really does suck, they refused to cover more than three days at a time. So on the third day, after spending the whole time there refusing to eat, I got to go home. Looking back, I should have gone back and signed myself in that very next day. Instead I became worse than when I'd gone in.

The next thing I remember my dad was at my house picking me up. I was just going to go with him for a few days. Somehow I wound up with a doctor in Indiana and a new therapist and this turned out to be a blessing. I was still throwing up every day. I was also now choosing to chase my antidepressant medication with alcohol, rather than taking it with water. The irony was being on my medication did have me binging and purging less. It just also made me not feel a need to eat at all, ever. Yet something in my head snapped in the next few months and I realized I wanted my life back. So in January I packed up and headed back out to Colorado.

I started eating and actually not purging all of the time. My new roommate and I wound up becoming good friends. Life was good. Yet, I still had that void there. So the eating disorder was still very much a part of my life. Then something happened that would change that entirely. I went home for my brother's wedding in June and found myself face to face with an old crush. Soon after that night we started dating. What's funny is at the time, loving anyone was the last thing on my mind. Yet, for whatever reason I decided to stay home, to stay with him. Suddenly, and quite unexpectedly, there was no void in my life. I did need to finish school and get a job, so things were still missing, but that overwhelming lonesome void that had been there for years was gone. From the day we started dating, I started eating better, or at least tried to, and I stopped purging all together. Occasionally I thought about it, but the thought left as quickly as it came. What breaks my heart is I know he was told otherwise. I also know, that I still looked sick at times and that made it easy to doubt me. Ultimately though, that love that we had saved my life. More than anything, I want him to know how thankful I am to him for that, even if things don't work out.

In the past year, I've had my moments. I do really well for a while and then do horribly for a while. Ultimately what I want is to be as healthy and happy as I was with him on my own. I'm finding new ways now to fill that void. For the first time in my life I'm doing things I enjoy, rather than just doing what I think needs to be done. Yet, lately, in all honesty, I am struggling. I love being on my own, but I miss home. Yet home is here and not there now. I like being on my own, but I get incredibly lonely at times too. I want the best of both worlds, to be able to do my own things, but to still be loved. I'm struggling every day with how bulimia is not the way to handle things. Even if it calms me down, the issues will still be there. I did okay for a while, so I know I can. What's funny is it didn't really hit me just how bad things are getting again until I sat down to write this. Talk about a major reality check. I have been told before that I am chronic and will never recover. A lost cause really. I happen to disagree and I plan on doing whatever it is I need to do to disprove that.

I'm done being sick. I'm done being healthy only to get sick again. This time, I want to get healthy and to stay that way, forever. A year ago I got a glimpse of how great life could be without an eating disorder. That's the sort of life I want for myself forever and for always.

3

Living with
Diabulimia

Everyday I have to make the choice between life and death. I know it sounds dramatic but it is true. Every injection brings with it guilt, a conscious decision to care for myself, but I ask you this, would you save someone you despised? Would you really pull them up from an existence you thought they deserved? It would be oh so easy just to let go and I have come close.

Eating disordered from a young age, fad diets, the idea set firmly in my mind that thin equaled good and there was far too much of me. As a rosy-cheeked girl with wonky eyes and a shy disposition, I was an easy target for name calling and playground disapproval. I usually sat in the corner of the classroom with my head down, hoping no one would call upon me. At the age of nine the warning signs came on, a healthy hue replaced by white skin, exhaustion, an insatiable thirst that kept me peeing every ten minutes or so. I was dehydrated, despite guzzling so much fluid and was dropping weight dramatically. My mother was, of course, worried and so took me to the doctors. From there it was straight into hospital, faced with the unfortunate diagnosis of type one juvenile diabetes. With this came confusion, I didn't understand why it had happened to me, what had I done wrong? I pushed it back, pretended it wasn't really happening. I hated the attention, the wide eyes in the physical education changing rooms when I ate a chocolate bar to give me sugar before sport, the "Oh I wish I could have snacks in lessons like you." From the very beginning it felt like a curse. My self-esteem fell to rock bottom.

I remember the time a girl a few years younger than me told me of how her mother had told her diabetes was caused by eating too much sugar. All too often type one and type two diabetes are not separated like they need to be as completely different illnesses. Even though I had been told of this and how only type two was brought on by obesity and eating the wrong foods, the fact that people might think that of me was terrifying and embarrassing. Along with the management of diabetes there was to be a certain amount of focus on food, diet, meal plans, what to eat and when. I had to see a nutritionist and count carbohydrates and test my sugars regularly. Also, with the aid of insulin, this so-called "medicine," I started to gain back the weight I had shed before and although I had no energy and felt terrible that consequence had been welcome.

I still wanted to lose weight. I always wanted to lose weight. I can't remember a time when this was not the case. I felt so uncomfortable and out of control as the numbers on the scale rose with age. As for when I discovered the deadly trick of skipping insulin to achieve such a result, I am not quite sure. I do wish I had never found out. The years since are hazy, snatches of memory revealing concerned glances and hospital visits, a blur of self-destruction, ongoing and painful. I restricted my intake and started to throw up when I felt I needed to. With unwanted revelation and attempts at intervention by those who cared about me I had to be more careful and eat under supervision. It was then I began to binge in secret and purge with shame numerous times a day.

In a few months' time I will be 21, and I have missed so much out of living. The things a typical teenager took for granted were impossible for me. Socializing and having fun can be so so difficult when you feel dead inside. People can see through the façade and know you are breaking, even if all you want to do is hide it, cover the scars, the red marks on your hands, and halt the tears. My last year of high school was patchy. I was absent more than present and in the end scrapped the last term as I could not summon the strength to even walk there in the mornings. I passed my GCSEs, with starred As in English and English Literature and having done no revision. I was proud, but as usual dwelled on the negatives – a D in Science, C in History, C in Art which was achieved with the aid of a medical note as my portfolio was not even finished. I lasted just two weeks at college, where I rushed around as a 71-pound ball of nerves. I was working constantly, throwing up everything I was eating, which wasn't much at all, and disguising the strong smell of ketones with chewing gum. My mother has always been able to tell when my sugars are raised simply by standing near me and recognizing that smell. At this point I crashed. I was sent to hospital, which I thought would be the weekend, after blood test results showed my liver and kidneys were struggling to function. This was a result of omitting my injections and surviving on as little insulin as I possibly could. Although upon learning this, the danger did not register. I was dumbfounded by the urgency and fuss, the words, "you might die" meaning nothing. They threatened to section me if I did not comply with further treatment at a specialist adolescent unit for anorexics and bulimics. I cried and fought and promised to get better if they let me go, but they would not. In the end I just had to give in.

But it did not work. I was the best patient, I did everything I was supposed to and propped everyone up with my positive advice and friendship. Inside though, I did not believe what I was saying at all. I stayed two months and then persuaded my mother to agree on a discharge. I just could not stand it anymore. I lied through my teeth with stories of what I was looking forward to once I was recovered, but I just wanted to starve myself again. They were making me fat and they were hopeless with my diabetic control. In my last therapy session they all but admitted that when I was asked, "So what should we do if we have to admit another diabetic patient in the future?" Within months I had gotten out of outpatient sessions and finally felt free.

The years roll into each other, with little change aside from the high frequency moments when I fall into danger. I have fallen into diabetic ketoacidosis at least three times, a condition caused by lack of insulin that has a 70 percent mortality rate. I have had a minor heart attack. I have been on antidepressants for a while now. My potassium is often too low from the amount that I throw up and my finances are a mess. This is something you rarely hear of in cases of bulimia, but the result can be disastrous and it has been for me. I have spent thousand of pounds buying food, indulging my habit at a turn of the head, all too often dwelling on a sign advertising café, takeaway or even pricy restaurant food: a means to fold into myself and lose myself in distraction, avoid the hectic pace of public life and find company in fresh sandwiches, pasta or iced buns.

I am now at university, but I am not too well. I went back to college part time and finished with two A levels. I was shocked to say the least, but relieved. Coming to university was the next logical step, something "normal" people would do and here I am still playing happy. I am balancing the eating disorder alongside my will to do well, to get my degree and make my family and friends proud. I am treading water and just about keeping my head above the tide. At the moment I confess I am struggling to learn more than the menus of everywhere in a five-mile radius. My concentration is awful and waking from the escape of sleep and getting to classes is often not possible. I have recently been in hospital again, but it was pointless seeing as it was merely a "refeeding unit" and had no therapy or group resources at all. It is just a plaster to press over a gaping wound that will peel away eventually, revealing a bloody mess. I only found this out after getting there and I felt so trapped, tricked. The trouble with my case is that it is unique, what with the diabetic complications aside anorexia with a purging subtype. A medical ward can regulate your blood sugars and an eating disorder ward can make you eat, but it is rare that anyone understands that the two come hand in hand and need to be treated together.

I would love to be able to conclude this in a positive way. Perhaps with a resolution, a description of what I have learned or what I am looking forward to. But the truth is, I cannot. There is no happily ever after, because I still struggle every day. Despite putting my body through so much abuse, I still cannot stop. I take more insulin than I used to and I try to stay out of ketoacidosis but I am still labeled as "emaciated," still purging too much and still cutting back on injections when I feel I need a "back-up" to my other weight-controlling habits. I do not really look forward, but around me, wondering when or how the damage will catch up with me. Organ failure, blindness, a loss of a limb or two, complete immobility, there are so many risks. I feel stupid, ridiculously stupid for still being sick, for fighting in a sense to keep starving and hurting myself. To a normal person I realize it just sounds insane, but it's my excuse, my way of accepting the fact that I am here and I am alive. I do this in order to let myself exist.

4

Surrounded by People but Completely Alone

If I ever need anything my family is there for me. Financial support, unexpected emergencies, earth-shattering events, apparently anything. Growing up I was never physically alone, or without company. I did learn, though, one could be very alone, even if the room is full of people. Let me put it this way, my family is Greek – and I mean Greek.

What does that mean? It means holidays weren't just my mother, father and the kids. It means the entire family, meaning humongous extended family, was always there, together for everything. Christmas was aunts, uncles, cousins, friends, sort of friends and some random Greek person who used to live in the same town of a great aunt's niece when she was ten years old who they happened to bump into on the street the other day (you get the point). Our get-togethers could have kept a catering company in business. Everything was done in packs and everything was about family and food. The focus was on who was bringing what side dish, who was or wasn't eating, who cooked, who didn't cook, who should go on a diet but at the same time having to eat everything so as not to be disrespectful. A tremendous amount of importance was based on the food aspect of our get-togethers.

This overemphasis was by no means a helpful dynamic in regard to my eating disorder. When food isn't just food and has a deeper meaning in the family then there is not a far stretch in regard to using eating and purging as a coping skill or to express feelings. I never really learned how to say how I felt because the notion of keeping the family together and protected was by far more important than petty and inconvenient things like feelings.

Food was a central part of the family. It represented love and what the family used to share their affection for each other. Physical fullness and hunger really had little, or anything, to do with what you did or did not eat. The better food was reserved for those who deserved it and you ate what was given to you, pretty much as an acceptance of the giver's love. If you didn't want to eat then you needed a reason and a real deal, solid reason. Saying you just ate was often seen as an excuse, but also brought on intense guilt when the interaction would become "Well just sit down... have a little... for me." In those moments the debate in my head was usually whose feelings are first.

The purging sort of snuck in as an almost natural addition to the food atmosphere of my family. I am not saying my family encouraged self-induced vomiting but there was definitely the sense that some things needed to be kept to yourself and that most of the time it would be better to give in to someone else rather than stand out. I think that, for me, I couldn't just choose to rebel (like some people) and say, "Screw this. I am doing my own thing." But at the same time I wasn't satisfied and didn't want to just do what I was supposed to do. Because I didn't really know a healthy middle ground I opted to be somewhat of a coward and pretend to go with the flow while rebelling in my own little way.

Purging came as a way to please both. It was secretly rejecting what I didn't want, without letting those around me know I didn't want what they thought I should have. I didn't want to show my difference and I didn't. Yet, I also slowly shut off as a person. A once dynamic child who spoke her mind often, I gradually shrunk down to a shell of a person. I didn't think I was truly the person people wanted me to be but I didn't want to show them who the true me was. So I pretended to be what other people wanted. However, the less I spoke up and the more of myself I hid, the deeper I got into the eating disorder and the more resentful I became of the family I was so desperately trying to please. I didn't think anyone would truly love me as I really was and I was so scared of being alone I pretended I wasn't me.

The actual importance of family and the intense need to keep the culture together and to flourish as a group was a constant reminder. Of course the premise of that idea is wonderful but the strict adherence to a very firm set of beliefs left little room for opposing opinions. Aside from the benefits or comforting aspects of reinforcing family values, there was a rather intense collective thinking that the family is the only group of people you could ever trust, ever. Anyone and everyone else was, "after your money," "trying to take advantage of you," "untrustworthy," "never caring for you." Now, this point of view is a legitimate and realistic approach to the world my family once knew when they emigrated from Greece to the United States. The views are practical and beneficial; family members help others. No matter how much a person put helping one in need before their own personal wants, friends outside the family were not trustworthy. While acquaintances are acceptable, the idea of actually opening up and being vulnerable to a non-family member could absolutely and often did have serious repercussions. Most importantly, you shouldn't really want your own space or to be alone because if you aren't comfortable saying or doing something around your family, chances were you were "doing something wrong."

The difficulty was, when I was growing up, I wasn't a stranger in a new country. I didn't need to worry about obtaining an education or finding enough food. I had a fairly standard American childhood. I wanted to play sports, hang out with friends and had grandiose rather than practical career aspirations. My needs were different and the things I wanted weren't just basic survival needs. My wants were more complex, perhaps less practical, and I just didn't know how to manage them. Even though I lived in a different time to my family, they were sort of stuck. I was told I needed to be successful, raise a family with a nice Greek boy, put others before myself, hold my tongue, be respectful and always be strong. There was this rigid mold that was often disguised as independence. The idea was that I could do what I want as long as it was the "right" thing. I could choose to go any way I wanted but at the same time if my wants were too different or too unconventional then I was no good, selfish, lazy and disrespectful for talking back. I was taught I needed to know what I wanted and to go after it, no matter what. Feelings and fears were pointless and needed to be put aside. Feelings were good or bad, a selfish thought made you a selfish person. Just thinking the wrong thing was almost as bad as actually doing the wrong thing. My thoughts, however, were different and I was ashamed of them because I thought it meant I was wrong.

The food became so important. It was the only time I would let myself go and be me. The more of myself I hid, the more fearful I became of the intense, burning and out of control desire. The purging was vital; not just throwing up but exercise too. I couldn't and I wouldn't let anyone see what sort of wanting monster I was. I wanted to be accepted but at the same time I wasn't even there. It was just an empty and numbed out human who was surrounded by people but completely alone. Let us just say that I felt an intense desire, a survival really, to protect myself from that terror in my stomach which grew stronger in relationships and with unexpected emotions. My entire eating disorder served to distract me from my fears, the panic in my stomach.

The strange thing is that this idea of mine, although working at first, slowly began to take on a life of its own. Of course now that I look back the transformation doesn't seem odd at all and really seems quite obvious. In the past when I may have been sitting at the table listening to my family scrutinize or emphasize on my behaviors I would have merely sat and quietly listened while eating the food I was supposed to. I would excuse myself and privately vomit up the food, the conversation and the feelings. After a while the patter changed. I would still sit there quietly listening but I started to be more aware of my frustration and anxiety. Instead of eating only what I was supposed to have I started to put my energy into eating faster and with the sole purpose of, quite literally, "puking my brains out." It didn't seem so quiet anymore and it's probably because I was feeling anger and didn't know how else to express it. You see I really do love my family and I just didn't know how to be mad or accept that everyone is different and that is okay.

Soon I realized that when I was home I rarely ate. I refused to give myself nourishment because, to me, it wasn't just food. It was always connected to these intense relationships. I wanted a break from the intensity, so I would completely take it away. I also noticed that while I ate little when I was away from home, when my family was around I would usually binge. I was eating more and purging, as if undecided. I wanted my family, the relationships and the support but I also feared the want. The binging and purging were a way to have both – to take more than I needed and then convince myself I was bad and greedy. I would convince myself I wanted too much, I was too dependent on my family. I couldn't just find some middle ground. The hard part would be acknowledging to myself and to my family that I wanted something more than what they had to offer. I wanted something different. I felt so selfish for that because by showing I wanted more would show they may not have enough. The benefit of tunnel vision is you don't know there is anything else and thus wouldn't miss it. By opening my eyes, and theirs, I risked making them feel unfulfilled or unable to change. I was terrified that acknowledging I may have different needs would mean I may need to branch away from my family. The conflict is I didn't want to risk being alone. I didn't know how to experience other relationships or trust other people. I was afraid that if I was different, if my family couldn't support me, then I would need to be alone. I would either have to be by myself and alone or not be the real me and stay stuck in that situation. I was afraid I'd either fly alone or be grounded and numb to the people around me.

I have slowly started to express these conflicts more and more as I've aged. I still have this intense and overwhelming need to be productive and to do the "right thing." I have an incredibly difficult time believing that anyone could care about me if I stopped being who they wanted and started being who I wanted. But I am learning. I have my boyfriend and I have real friends. Now, I know that sounds strange but I never thought I could have anyone care about me if they saw me when I was not giving them what they wanted. I'm trying to be gentle with myself and to be thankful for having my close-knit and loving family, but also acknowledging that it is okay if I need my own space as well. It seems as I've slowly moved away from the intensity and mandatory family obligations I have started to enjoy talking, really talking with my family. It seems that when I am not myself I can be in a room surrounded by people and feeling all alone. But, when I am being true to myself I can be physically alone but emotionally feel more connected than I have ever felt in my life.

5

Running Away but Going Nowhere

Sometimes, you don't know how bad something is until you take a small break from it. Sometimes, you can convince yourself you are a machine and that you, and only you, have to keep going. Sometimes, you convince yourself of this because the idea of reaching out and showing how vulnerable and unmachinelike you are is scarier than being stuck in your own revolving, manipulating, continuous mind spin. My own system of management, no matter how seemingly bizarre and pointless, was clearer and safer to me than the chaos of my feelings and of relationships; or perhaps just clearer than trying to make sense of them. What was this system of mine? Well, it was my eating disorder of course.

I cannot quite explain what it was I so greatly feared. For some reason feelings brought about a terror within the gut of my stomach, which would paralyze me if not taken care of immediately. I cannot pinpoint exactly where those fears stemmed from. I can claim, maybe, on the surface what it was that I was so deeply terrified of, but I know I just don't quite understand it.

I can pretend the fear was because I felt horrible or because I could not show myself to others. Perhaps I was certain I could never show myself to others and my very human vulnerabilities were atrocious. I didn't quite believe this but there was no other reason I could think of, of why I would resist with all my might to show my humanity to others. Even though I wasn't sure why, I was not going to take chances. So it was, and is, safer to make an ultimate reason to why I must protect and hide myself. I had no patience for myself or for uncertainty.

With the eating disorder, I finally understood how I could live a life that was entirely expected and self-contained, while giving the illusion of something else. It wasn't that I would pretend the horror in my stomach didn't exist, nor would I ignore it. Instead I would use my eating disorder, specifically the bulimia, and exercise to soothe and appease the feelings while not showing the extreme distress occurring in my mind to anyone. They say the eyes are the windows to the soul. My eyes were boarded up and the eating disorder was what kept everyone out and kept me dark and alone. I pretended to be an empty and abandoned house. But instead I was a ghost stuck in a house that would slowly collapse inwards. If the boards did not come off, then the very house protecting the ghost of me would cease to exist. For what use is an abandoned house, if no one can ever get in or out?

My eating disorder went through many phases in its development over more than half of my 22 years. Perhaps the most intriguing, gripping, manipulative, provocative, repetitive, cyclical and adaptive was the exercise. It engulfed me. Exercise was my outlet, my time, my punishment, but also my gift. It was so important for me to exercise. I did anything to keep it alive. Initially I started with the rather simple fantasy of wanting to lose weight. I limited food and increased the exercise. There is only so long a body can endure restricting and exercising so at a crucial point I had to choose what part of the eating disorder was most essential. Sure I claimed I wanted to be thin, no matter what, but in the crossroad I knew the path for thinness was a dead end road. It would only get so far before being noticed, either by the diminishing body size, food avoidance or health consequences. I knew the temporary attention would be appealing, but even then I subconsciously knew it wouldn't give me what I truly wanted or needed. I wanted, instead, a way to perpetually take care of and manage myself. I created a never ending and familiar security around me.

Exercise was my life, not sports but exercise. I was never quite good enough to enjoy playing sports. I wanted to, I wanted to be the best runner, score the most baskets or be able to have enough skill to actually enjoy the social and satisfying aspects of athletics. I wanted, at the very least, to be good enough that I didn't have to feel like I needed to pre-apologize for my almost certain mediocre performance. I often would joke around, laugh it off, pretend it wasn't that big a deal or that I wasn't really determined or trying. But the determination was there and I was trying. The talent, however, was not. I couldn't be good enough, I couldn't fit in and the more I tried the worse I failed and the more embarrassed and isolated I became. I was always taught, "If you work hard enough for what you want then you will get it." My athletic mediocrity wasn't accepted and shrugged off like most people who discover and admit to a weakness in certain areas. Instead the sense of failure shifted as a protection to "I don't want to play with you, anyways!"

Perhaps I did not understand the idea of pleasure for itself. Enjoyment had to make sense, if I didn't have a reason to enjoy something then I couldn't. Why would I? Could I? Should I? My mind would jump around like an endless crazed bird with a broken wing. There I go trying to sound poetic again. Why did I feel the need to add some sort of clichéd metaphor? Do I think the metaphor will make my words appear more appealing? To fluff the paragraph with descriptive words rather than just directly saying what it is I want to say. Thoughts and ideas spring up and then collapse before they even can develop. That is what is happening now. My brain, trying to tell and explain an experience, cannot rest long enough to just let me say, or feel. Instead I am getting lost in what I am trying to say, because for some reason I need to make you, or someone, understand. Why? Why must someone understand? Why does it matter? As I sit struggling to find the words I feel myself closing off and agreeing to take the loss of "I have no freaking idea how to write this which is why no one will have any damn idea of what I am saying." Of course, I should point out, although that was my original thought I nearly put in an overly dramatic and certainly not me way of describing the same thought which would have been "I know not how to write... thus why I cannot say what I mean." I guess this is just another way I have of denying being who I am and instead trying to present myself in a way I think other people would find more "correct." Of course, this also loses any genuine "me-ness." But, for some reason I feel I need to pretty-fy my feelings. Yes, I am creating new words to describe my thoughts because I can't really think of any real ones that will get the point across.

The notion of enjoying something I was not particularly good at felt absurd. It was an embarrassment I refused to sit with. So I made myself change what I wanted. Changing or at least trying to change my wants became a pattern that engulfed other aspects of my life. I convinced myself I didn't care what people thought of me or that I wasn't interested in art. I didn't need help or attention. I lied. I lied to myself. I lied to the person I truly was because I did not want to realize my faults and potential failures. But, feelings don't change just because they are inconvenient. My feelings were simply rechanneled. All my guilt, anger, ambition and sadness were funneled into the eating disorder. I could deal with all the feelings on my own and in my mind, successfully.

The exercise created its own chaos. I understood the confusion of how my mind responded to my life and how exercise could adjust and mold the feelings in a more manageable or concrete way. Adaptive, maladaptive, habit, schedule, go, forward, more, not enough, lazy, weak, tired, too bad, faster, less, more, all – just all. These thoughts can keep you the same. It keeps me the same. They play and jump to each other round and round, never taking a break. They mean staying within me, within my own confusing but perfectly clear world. It's amazing how confusion can actually be understood and embraced, even when it really makes little sense. What does it mean to make sense? Is there a sense? I had to know. Maybe, that was my quandary – that I needed to understand, I had to know, I couldn't just be. Isn't that what control is about anyways? To always know what will come next, or what will not? I had a strong desire to make sense, of something, anything, and if the sense I chose was an absurd and delusional system created and functioning only in my mind then it would have to do. My system would do until I found what it was I was trying to make sense of in the first place.

I ate enough so I could exercise more. Free time meant exercise time because I had created an illusion I would go somewhere with it. But, I knew this was a lie. The point was to go and go and go, but never move forward. If every moment created the solution of exercise then the distraction of failure in other ways could be avoided. The lie was I wanted to lose weight and the solution was to exert more than I was eating. But really I wanted to distract, to exercise and to numb myself out. I didn't want to feel I wasn't letting myself live and I did not want to sit with myself. I couldn't sit with myself. I ate, I binged and then claimed I wanted to lose weight in order to exercise, to force myself to disconnect. Slight indulgences or major indulgences made the necessity of exercise unquestionable.

The rationalization, the waste of time all were reinforced by my self-imprisonment, self-sabotage. "I'm not that thin, I don't restrict that much, I don't purge that much. My problem is that I want to eat too much. The exercise is permission; it allows me to be healthy."

I sit here writing this on a park bench on a windy June day. I have just left a doctor's appointment where we discussed the physical consequences of my eating disorder, specifically the muscle and possible liver damage done by my exercise abuse; not to mention how the exercise exasperates the potential physical complications done by other aspects of my eating disorder. The constant pounding when I run increases my risk of bone damage, being that since I have a history of irregular menses my bones are already more prone to harm. The dehydration from the exercise further increases the danger I faced with electrolyte imbalances due to constant purging, as well as laxative abuse. For so long I fooled myself in thinking that while the exercise was definitely a distraction from difficult feelings it could not possibly result in physical consequences. I now know I was kidding myself, but the sad part is I still cannot truly take it in. The difficulty comes in the constant repetitive thoughts that exercise is good, therefore more exercise is better. I know the inability for me to take in the potential dangers, despite ample evidence, which shows how ingrained and warped my thought processes have become.

I am on my way to my therapist's office to continue discussing the distraction that has become my life. The walk from my doctor is three miles on cobblestone. I have wedge shoes and a heavy bag, "click, clock, click, clock?" Is that the sound my shoes make? I don't even know. I have no idea what sound my shoes make against the pavement because even though I am always walking I never actually listen to myself, or feel it. It can't be "click, clock, click, clock." That isn't a realistic sound, walking isn't so smooth and predictable that the only sounds it makes are two syllables endlessly repeating. But that is the sound that came in my mind when it came to describe the sound of my shoes on the ground. It sounds like a clock, the "tick, tock" of the clock. Maybe I think I am walking around, walking like a clock, being a clock, using time? Wasting time? Or maybe I think that like the tick, tock ensures the continuation and certainty of the path of time I assume that the click, clock of my shoes ensures the continuity of me.

What am I even saying? "Click, clock" isn't even the sound of anything walking. It isn't even a real sound. Nothing sounds that smooth and simple, especially something moving over an uncertain and uneven ground. The cracks, the bumps, the people, the stops, they all change the sound and the supposed familiar and expected sounds of a walk. I want to pretend I can describe the sound of my shoes on the ground. I want to pretend I know the sounds of walking, passing, whatever, through life. But, I don't. How long will I pretend I know the sound of my shoes on the ground? How long will I pretend I can actually repeat the same familiar, identical, pattern over and over again? How long can I pretend there is even a recognizable pattern? Being in my head so much brings on such frustration. Now, I can't even imagine my simple walk is really that simple. When will I just accept I'll need to just feel my way through the unexpected streets, of New York, of life and of myself?

I have a stream of thoughts rushing through my head. It is a struggle to just take a break, just to relax. I tell myself, I should be walking to the gym and I should be running instead of wasting time with my pathetic attempts at writing. I lie to myself and claim it is perfectly rational to run in my spare time. If I am doing nothing significant I should at least be exercising so I don't show how truly lazy and worthless I feel. These are the convictions racing through my mind when I try to break away from my rigid belief system. I haven't run for a week, my longest, for a long time. I haven't run so my doctor can do blood tests, but now they are done. I should run, I need to run. My fat ass is obligated to run. But, I'm not. Strangely the week off didn't allow me a chance to be more rested. It instead showed me how used to my extreme exhaustion I was. Sitting here, writing this, has taken more energy than all the hours and all the miles of running.

I was and still am terrified of the unknown. Of not knowing what to expect of moving on, so I didn't go anywhere I didn't already understand. If you are never going anywhere you don't need to think of what will happen when you get there. I lived a life of a subhuman nature, passing for normal. The weight was on the low side but rarely dropped past a certain point. The need to exercise had to remain and it did. I wasn't interested in using the eating disorder as some sort of finite solution. I knew there was no pot of gold at the end of the rainbow. I knew the search and journey would truly get me nowhere and thus waste time and energy. But, that is what I desired. I wanted to waste time under the illusion it was progress. I didn't want to reach the end of the road and then find out there was nothing there. So like the treadmill I endlessly walked. I forced myself to keep moving and moving, towards a false goal but truly going nowhere. I wasn't going forward in life or forward in the eating disorder.

The exercise bulimia contained me and hid my desires from the world. I truly felt I had the perfect distraction. My body wouldn't hurt from the eating disorder, no one would notice and I could deal with everyday life. However, my body did begin to hurt. I did want someone to notice, even if I denied needing or wanting any help. Although I could get through a normal life, I wasn't really living it. I wasn't experiencing life because for some reason I felt the purpose was only the end goal, the final product. It is interesting how I felt life's purpose was to get to some sort of end goal and your experience was not necessary. Yet, with exercise I thrived on the experience and never truly tried to reach the end point, whatever it may have been. I only lived or experienced my exercise.

Despite the idea that I need to "take it easy" I still can't shake the need to walk. In fact I curse myself for taking the time to sit and write this. I fear I do not exist if I am not moving. Frustration, agitation, words and words and words. Which word is the right word? Which word explains me? Why can't I find it and why am I searching so hard for just the word that explains it all? It doesn't exist.

6

A Love
of Athletics

I'm not sure where my drive to win has come from, but it was instilled in me at a very early age. Ever since I could remember, I was out on the tennis courts, swinging rackets that seemed bigger than me, begging my mother for "five more minutes." I remember telling her that I would eat in the car, since we were going to be late to horseback riding, to swim team, to gymnastics, to any number of lessons that I took. Those early days, I loved sports. I loved the sound made with my racket when I hit a hard backhand from the baseline. I loved seeing my competitor chase down the ball, only to sometimes return it successfully.

Hearing the gun go off at the start of swim meets, that often went late into the night, those nights were special. All of my school friends were in bed and my swim friends and I, we were allowed to stay up, because we had to, for the team.

I loved the quiet trotting of my pony during an early Saturday morning lesson. Hearing that because I was such a good rider, I got to go on a trail ride, or stay after and practice jumps.

I loved the innocent days of sports, where they were about camaraderie and companionship and not about calories or the most time spent at the gym.

As I grew, as most girls are wont to do at some point in their lives, my body began to change and that affected my sports. I wasn't running as fast on the court. My lap times weren't as fast. I wasn't as light in the saddle. People began to notice and I began to freak out. What was I going to do? At this early stage in my life, I had no clue what healthy eating was. Sure, we ate healthy at home and stayed away from fast food. My insecurities began to override my judgment and I wondered if I really was eating healthy. My thoughts were confirmed, when, at the age of 12, at five feet and two inches and 98 lbs, I stopped home from tennis practice to grab an extra practice outfit since I had to be up at the pool for swim practice shortly, then I had another tennis practice right after and my mother, as I'm grabbing an apple, says, "That tennis skirt makes you look pregnant, maybe it's time we gave it away."

I never swam so hard in my life as I did in the following practice. I can also say my heart wasn't in it 100 percent. I felt betrayed, to say the least. Leaving the pool feeling dejected, I walked over to the tennis courts, changed and began practice. After practice was over, I ran laps around the courts to punish myself for not being a good athlete, a good person and a good daughter.

"Why are you late for dinner? You know what time dinner starts," my mother says as I walk in the door from practice that evening. I told her that a couple of us had stayed after to practice. As I sat down, she admonished me for putting too much on my plate. Even now, 12 years later, I still see carbohydrates as the enemy. I didn't realize then that a half-cup of rice with some steamed vegetables was "bad."

The next morning, I suddenly became thankful that my brother and I had long since been responsible for packing our own lunches. Coming from a family where both parents work, my mother had decided that once we were old enough to start taking items out of our lunch that we didn't like, we were old enough to start making our own lunch. Instead of the usual veggie sandwich on wheat bread, apple or carrot sticks and some trail mix, in went some cucumber slices, some carrot slices, an apple and two bottles of water. I helped my younger brother pack his lunch so it resembled more of a lunch and not an entire package of sandwich cookies and off we went.

"It's doughnut day at school, Mother," I said, when she yelled down the stairs inquiring about breakfast. "And Andrew had cereal, like he always does."

On the ride to school, I can't help fidgeting and noticing that the other girls look so thin in their uniforms. Granted, knee-length pleated plaid doesn't look good on anyone, but it looks hideous on me. The younger kids get dropped off at the lower school and the woman in charge of carpool that day parks to walk us in. It seems like the only thing I can notice is all the thin girls; girls that were not this thin the previous Friday.

Classes seem a blur, as all I can do is think about losing weight. I keep my stomach clenched as much as possible during the day. I do leg lifts under the desk to keep moving. When lunchtime comes, I am filled with both anticipation and dread. I quickly find a seat with my friends and then realize I can't eat this lunch in front of them. All-girls' schools are a breeding ground for gossip. If I simply say that we ran out of all-wheat, seven-grain bread this morning, the whole school would know it by the time lunch was over. Since this clearly wasn't the case, this was not something I wanted getting back to my mother, which, it would by English class at the latest. I nibble on some of my food, finding myself thinking of when I'll be home alone, when I can eat in peace. Lunch ends without too much commotion.

Back at home a couple hours later, I am ravenous. I also need to get my homework at least started before tennis practice, because it won't get done between that and swim practice. Or was it gymnastics I had today? I look at the calendar on the fridge. Good, it's gymnastics, that gives me extra time to do my homework. I grab a bowl of cereal and head upstairs with my overflowing backpack. Once my homework is mostly done, I find that I have extra time before gymnastics. I contemplate going over to the library to research dieting as, yes, I am that clueless. The only magazines we had around the house were about golfing and homes and gardens, neither of which offered up any great insight. This was the day of the emerging internet, when free internet disks were given out everywhere. Of course you had to own a computer and have an internet connection, so my brother and I just kept the free disks that we accumulated at an alarming rate and waited for the day when we too could join the millions of others on the World Wide Web.

I decide to do some simple push-ups and sit-ups, as coach has us do them sometimes in gymnastics as a warm-up. Then I add jumping jacks. When I felt my heart start to race, I got giddy. "Maybe this is what working out is," I think to myself. "Maybe all those other times didn't count, because it never felt this good!"

My ride comes to take me to practice and I wonder how I'll feel. Will it be different, knowing that I've already gotten a "workout" in for today? At the gym, things proceed as normal. I'm a bit lightheaded, having barely eaten anything all day, but I push through and figure I just haven't had enough water. In the locker room at the end of practice, I hear one of the senior girls talking about how she's gained weight and another girl telling her to just throw up, she'll be fine. The senior girls get weighed and I know from overhearing them in the locker room that it scares them. I only get weighed when I go to the doctor and she always tells me I'm healthy, so it doesn't scare me, but maybe healthy isn't good.

That night at dinner I can't get the conversation out of my mind. What did she mean, "just throw up?" She didn't look like she had the flu. Suddenly I understood. I quickly excused myself from the table and went upstairs, flipped up the toilet lid, slid two fingers down my throat and up came dinner. I cleaned up the bathroom, brushed my teeth and got ready for bed. "I have more homework to do," I told my mother, "so I'm going to bed early."

Fast forward to age 24. Outpatient therapy started at 17, two hospitalizations later at 22 and 23 and I'm binging and purging on up to 40,000 calories daily. I have osteoporosis in my hips and no enamel left on my teeth. My love of sports had continued throughout the years, ranging from a love for the sport, to a way to burn calories and fuel the eating disorder. I started triathlon training in 2006. I fell in love with the camaraderie, the sport, the intenseness all over again. I didn't dare tell any of the coaches or other girls about my eating disorder "history" for fear of what would happen and continued to train like everyone else.

Early fall 2007 I began to notice a nagging pain in my left shin. I wrote it off as shin splints and continued local five-kilometer runs on the weekends, swim workouts in the mornings and bike workouts in the evenings. The pain began to get worse, despite some rest and self-care. After briefly speaking to one of the girls after a five-kilometer run in which I did horribly, I decided to seek out the advice of a physician. Upon hearing my history and doing an exam, we came to the conclusion that it was a stress fracture. "So, reduce my mileage a bit, right, since it's not a complete break," I said, knowing full well that this is not what she had in mind.

"No running for 30 days." I think I passed out. No running? Doesn't she understand that it's what I live for? It's what gets me out of bed in the morning, it's what keeps me in shape, it's what I have in common with "normal" people, people who don't do sick things with their food. What would I do without it? Surely I would revert way back into my old eating disorder habits. She put me in a walking cast and then we sat down to talk seriously about my eating disorder. She wants me to consider going in-patient somewhere. "But I've already been," I begin to protest earnestly.

"You need somewhere long term," she said, "somewhere that will actually allow you to exercise and teach you to do it in a healthy manner. Somewhere that has several components to their program, so when you come back home, you are functional and ready to begin your life as a healthy athlete."

I began to cry. Not only was she taking away my running, but she was also telling me I should give up my life. The rational side of me says that this is the best time to go into treatment, when you can barely walk, because that's when I'll get the most out of groups instead of trying to plan ways to run around without staff noticing. This eating disorder has taken away 12 years of my life so far. There is no ending to this story. I am still broken and beginning to mend. My nights are still filled with major binge and purge sessions. My days are filled with sleep and whatever workouts I can figure out with this cast on my leg. I have given so much to my eating disorder and all it has given me is physical and emotional pain. Little by little, step by step, I will reclaim my life and be back out there, in the pool, on the tennis courts, pounding the pavement, spinning my wheels. This time, just a little bit healthier.

7

Recovery or What Passes for Normal

By definition, I am no longer bulimic. An identity I have held, nurtured, fought against and defined myself by has passed away. To be fair, I do still purge. I have been at this point between diagnosably disordered and in recovery for a little over a year. But about once every month, every two months, I eat "too much" and I feel "too full" and I pull myself towards a bathroom and forcibly empty myself. During finals week, I binged and purged three times on a Monday when the stress broke me. But aside from these slips, I eat well. I do not diet, I watch what I eat but only to judge my hunger and "need." I do not deny myself desserts or carbohydrates or French fries. I eat plenty of fruits and vegetables, but I order pizza with my roommate without thinking and without purging. I am what many call recovered and I cannot believe this.

In order to understand the significance and ramifications of this absence, I need to preface it with the past and the truth. At age 12, I began my dive into eating disorders. Anorexia subsumed my depression and anxiety and whittled me into something too small. I did not see a doctor or a therapist until 16, when my mother brought me to a social worker for weekly therapy. Around then, I began to teach myself to purge at moments of weakness. It was a deep secret.

During the winter break from school, I forced myself into an extended fast. When I broke the fast, I found myself unable to stop eating. My "lessons" came in handy. I fell head first into bulimia. I moved quickly from my normal rituals of starvation to multiple binge and purge sessions a day. I turned 17. A few days after my birthday, I began intensive treatment after a suicide attempt. The treatment, in the form of two hospital stays and two day programs, lasted until the beginning of my senior year of high school. Despite the efforts of doctors, therapists and nurses, my desire to remain bulimic kept me purging just enough to meet the clinical definition for bulimia. It was important for me to keep the label on my forms. I feared the notion of being ignored and discounted because I did not have an identifiable problem. I could not let my therapist, my family or my friends forget me. Bulimia desperately kept me noticeable and significant. Mostly, though, it was impor-tant I recognized I had some sort of problem. Again, despite the efforts of all involved in that spring/summer of treatment, my depression had not lifted. It was not enough for me, though, to feel sad; I desired some sort of proof I felt this way and that something was wrong with me. I have not yet mentioned any of my "circumstances" or "environ-ment," the complex net of social and familial and biological and everything factors, but it is necessary at this point. My father has, and has had, a terminal illness for the past decade. Every day he grows more and more ill. Today, he can neither walk nor speak and he has 24-hour home care. Back then, though, he was only beginning to use a wheelchair. My sadness, my depression, held none of the physical issues. Anyone could look at my dad and see his suffering. Mine was inside. The need for "proof," then, became paramount in my mind. I could not call myself sick when a grade-A example of illness lived with me. The raw physicality of bulimia validated my pain to myself. I needed to remain bulimic.

Of course, I did not binge and purge only to prove to myself I was sick; rather, that is why I wanted the identity of 'bulimic' so badly. Binging and purging held many benefits in my mind; foremost was I could eat without keeping the calories (over which I obsessed). My weight at this time was between slightly underweight and the low end of normal, without much fluctuation, and I believed bulimia kept me in that range. I needed the outlet. I was an achiever in high school, with straight As, French club, drama club and the debate team. I could go on about the reasons I continued to binge and purge, but at this point, habit and dependence played highly into the disease.

Once school started, I returned with renewed vigor to binging and purging. Between September and March, I consistently purged between three and ten times a day. Bordering suicidal and miserable, I also burned or cut myself daily and was drinking alcohol and using a variety of drugs (cocaine, amphetamines and painkillers). I remember this time in all my senses, the coolness of the tile in my bathroom where I occasionally collapsed (involuntarily or because I simply could not bring myself to stand), the anxiety as I microwaved cheese onto crackers and the 20-second interim before eating, the songs I chose especially for vomiting. To be honest, it all blurs together and in my mind, the period was much shorter than it ever felt or really was. I prefer not to go to the place in my head that led to the physical and mental anguish. I am unable to recount this time without shaking.

On 7 March, at 17, in my senior year of high school, I entered a residential treatment center 20 minutes south of my family's home. I remained there for 100 days. I purged four times while at the facility. The dramatic decrease had simple reasons. I felt unable to purge. A staff member took me to the bathroom (and I had to have the door open) every time for the first 60 days. I wanted to stop. I was finding other outlets for the needs that led me to purge. I was greatly invested in pleasing people and not purging did that.

The treatment was costly. To this day, I am ashamed of how much money has been spent on me because of my disorders. Treatment also cost me the end of my senior year of high school, my senior prom and many things I mourn still. Good things did happen there. I found a combination of medications that kept my depression and anxiety manageable. I met friends I still have today, almost two years later. I grew into myself, my boisterous, giggly self rather than my sick, depressed self. I graduated, through self-study, from high school and received acceptance letters to nine colleges. But two days after I left the facility for a summer at home, I purged. A week later, I started using drugs again, this time cocaine and heroin. I was purging two or three times a day and using drugs throughout the summer. That September, last September, I left for a college 600 miles away. I stopped using drugs, but immediately fell into a combination of restricting and purging that drove off all of the weight I had gained in treatment and more. I was depressed as badly as, if not worse than, before and I stopped taking my medication. It was a very bad time and I am not sure if it is because it is so recent or because of the scale of the sadness that makes it so tangible to me. But a month-long winter break at home with my friends and family, combined with medication and therapy, brought me to a much sunnier spring semester and what would start this period of stasis.

I do not mean to rush through my history. It confuses most when I try to retell it and even I lose track sometimes of specific incidents, what happened, where it happened, when? The quick oscillations of my mental state and eating disorder do not always proceed logically. But I do not believe the past is important, in this context, except to demonstrate where I have been and what I have done. This is the sum, I have been sick for about eight years. I have been through a handful of treatment programs. I have been very sick and not-so-sick and right now people sometimes call me recovered.

Right now I am nearly 20 and in my second year of college. I have a job and a good grade point average. I have friends and a boyfriend. I take medicine every day to keep my brain stable. I do not use drugs. Comparatively, I am golden. I have what I wanted and what I strove for. My field of study, international affairs, has been a passion for years and there's no reason I can't or won't have a bright future.

A part of me, though, says if this is recovery, they lied to me. I wanted a recovery where I would never feel the imperative, undeniable need to purge. I wanted a recovery where I wouldn't have to take pills every day. I wanted a recovery where I was recovered, goddammit, not where I still had the option and specter of purging behind me. "They," meaning the psychiatrists, psychologists, social workers, nurses, everything, had never said I would have to purge some days and not others. They never said when I would have to be truly miserable and incapable of moving some days. And here is where my thoughts diverge. Maybe a full recovery is not and never will be possible for me, maybe it's not for anyone. Maybe I'm not recovered at all, just a different kind of sick and I don't know it. Maybe I'm not trying hard enough to not be sad. I don't know, I'm not sure if I can know. But the startling appearance of bulimic tendencies every so often alternately frightens me and comforts me. I am so familiar with the rhythm of eating and vomiting. I am terrified of going back to vomiting a half dozen times a day. When people call me recovered, I am scared though, because that term means this is it, this is recovery and so I will always be stuck on this slope.

So, then, what am I? I'm not clinically bulimic, but I still semi-regularly engage in bulimic behavior. I'm not recovered, but my eating is normalized for the most part. For so long, I have classified and judged my life by my weight, my calorie intake, the number of times I have purged, what medications I have been taking, what diagnoses I have. Even when I play other roles, captain of the debate team, for example, bulimia has supplemented and backed these. I don't have an answer. I have not let go of bulimia, I am not sure if I can. My life has improved in many ways, but the past reminds me just how easily I could begin binging and purging right now. I could effortlessly fall into a pattern of self-destruction. At this point, I believe the inertia of almost a year keeps me mostly healthy, but maybe it's something else. The notion

I may live in this state of limbo looms in my mind. I have plans for the future and I have hope. Will I still be throwing up when these dreams are realized? Is this it?

8

High-functioning Superwoman

At 22 years old, I was a high-functioning, eating-disordered woman. I'd spent a hot, long summer starving myself in Texas during an intense training period for my job as an Intel troop in the United States Air Force. Finished with training, I unpacked my bags in a foreign country and prepared to enjoy myself. I couldn't wait to go clothing shopping here. It was my first time in Asia and I knew from my friends there were many stores catering to very petite women.

When my routine weigh-in came up, the Air Force weighs you on a regular basis, I didn't expect there to be a problem with my being underweight. But I was referred to a doctor on base who told me that unless I could maintain a weight over a BMI of 18 he would have to diagnose me as anorexic and send me back to the States. I didn't want to go. I was adamant there was nothing wrong with my eating habits. "I am certainly not anorexic, I just like being small. My weight fluctuates," I said, but he listened to nothing. I thought, "I'll show him." So I ate, and I ate. And the eating was stressful, I couldn't be alone with it. I threw out the scale. I went out, every night, with coworkers, with *anyone*, and I drank, which made eating easier. I didn't want to go home alone, so I went home with men, and women, I barely knew. There was nothing wrong with me. How could I be an uptight anorexic? I ate, drank and made merry seven nights a week. I had a reputation, not as a drunk or a slut, but as a party girl who always had a good time. My clothes from Texas didn't fit, but I didn't care. Hell, I was under 100 pounds in Texas, I reminded myself. Now I'm normal.

Until I decided I needed a new pair of jeans. I headed to a local clothing store idly wondering what my size now was. I don't try on clothing in dressing rooms, I always take them home to try on and this time was no different. I figured I couldn't be any larger than a size nine, so I bought the same jeans in a nine and a seven and went home to try them on. The nines didn't even fit over my thighs. I didn't think anything. I just went and took a nap.

When I woke up, everything had changed. Party girl? Monster. Look at me. How could I have missed this? This fatness? I looked at photos of myself from less than a year before. Tiny. I had gained some 50 to 60 pounds. I was overweight. Well overweight. I had a weigh-in coming up. Calmly I looked in the mirror and thought, "800 cals a day. Done it before, this will be gone soon. Just get through a few weeks, that's all." I stopped going out. I stopped drinking. Nothing was more important than getting my weight back to a normal range. My cell phone was turned off. I lay in bed and imagined eating food while I chewed sugar-free gum. I had done all this before, but this time it hurt. It hurt because my body was so much bigger, so much *hungrier* than it had ever been and I hated my body for it. I

couldn't sleep because of the hunger. I went to the psychiatrist on base and asked for sleeping medication. He gave it
to me. It relaxed me, but it couldn't cut through the
hunger to put me to sleep. Still, it was something. I looked
forward to taking it until the night when it relaxed me so
much that I thought, "Tonight I can eat something substantial, can't I?"

There was nothing in my dorm room that qualified as
substantial, really. There were cartons of skimmed milk,
apples, tuna and lettuce. Then I remembered the case of
"meals ready to eat" in my closet. These are the modern day
version of C-rations, very high calorie, fortified foods,
vacuum packed for deployed soldiers. I tore into one and
ate a packet of Spanish rice. It was the first time in months I
had broken my restriction. I was down to 120 pounds at
that time. This was a healthy weight for me, I realize now,
but I had never stopped seeing myself as 170 pounds and
now was no different. Horrified, I looked in the mirror. I
was gaining it back. It was all going to come back. How
weak of me.

"Some anorexic I turned out to be," I thought. I hated
that doctor. There was nothing wrong with me and he said
there was and then I'd gotten fat. But thinking about
anorexia brought up another thought. I didn't have to let
the rice make me fat. I could puke it up, like a bulimic, I
thought. I didn't really think it would work. I had tried
purging before, a few times in my life, but found I couldn't
overcome my own disgust with the act enough to relax and
let my gag reflex work. I was more pissed off than anything
else and thought, again, "I'll show him." I pulled the brown
plastic spoon out of the ready-to-eat meal bag and marched
into the bathroom, bent over the toilet and shoved it down

my throat. Nothing happened for a few minutes. I kept at it, not really thinking about anything but my anger. And then I found the sweet spot, the spot that worked for me then and still does today, and the contents of my stomach hurtled up my throat, over the back of my tongue and into the toilet.

It was supposed to be a one-time thing. But every night the medication would cut into my willpower, my compulsive hold over my hunger. Every night I would break down and eat. The first few times I still felt some horror but soon I began to look forward to it. I would plan my evening meal all day. Takeout? Elaborately cooked meals for one? Was it a night of pastries or candy or six different kinds of children's cereals? I'd rent movies. It became a party for myself every evening, sitting on the floor in my pajamas, watching movies from home, shoveling food down and then throwing it back up. The weight came off – 120, 110, soon I was back to 100. The psychiatrist on base was thrilled. "Stopped stress eating, I see?" he'd joke. I'd grin, "Yes, I'm much happier now."

For a few months I was happy, until I started gaining weight again. Back up to 115, I panicked. What if I gained it all back? Soon it was not about eating healthily during the day and binging and purging at night. I restricted all the time, no more binges. But I purged everything, too. Purging made me hungrier though, and I lost control of my eating. Always eating, always purging. I couldn't get my weight below 110 and it would fluctuate ten pounds or more from day to day. I started drinking again. It was so easy to binge and purge when drunk. I realized I wasn't purging "like" a bulimic. I *was* a bulimic.

Five years later, I have broken the cycle of binging and purging. I purge on rare occasions now, every six months or so. But over the past five years my eating disordered behaviors have become increasingly more my master. Every time I avoid a purge, I must compensate with some other punishment. I am still "high functioning." I am 27, with a happy marriage, a good career, an education. I am respected and admired for my intelligence and intensity at work. "Superwoman" my boss calls me. I am bilingual. I have hobbies. I have talent. I have everything. But I still cry, every day, about food. Every time I sit down to eat, I wonder if it will be a binge. I track my calories. I write hundreds of pages in my journal weighing the pros and cons of eating this or that, of what I will "do" to lose more weight. I am under 100 pounds again. I still fluctuate a lot, between 95 and 115. I have tried treatment, but I have never believed in it. I will always remember that I lost control. I will always be afraid to lose it again.

I will probably never develop an eating disorder 'acute' enough to gain the notice that emaciated teenagers get. I am almost 30 now. I am petite to begin with and even at 95 pounds people only cluck their tongues and say I need a bit more meat on my bones. I am too driven and ambitious in other parts of my life to allow myself to end up bedridden. My obsession will always be invisible and I realized a long time ago it's too late for me to ever get better. I do the best I can each day. I manage my health as best I can, with my broken teeth, my chronically low blood pressure, my absurdly low blood sugar and my screwy hormone production. Every few weeks I carefully, precisely adjust my eating routine, not really hoping for improvement anymore, just some peace.

9

The Hardest part is Wanting to Recover

I sit in front of the television with the sound blaring, so I'm not faced with what I'm doing in silence. I don't have to think or worry. I savor the first few bites and then there is no enjoyment in the food. The food is greedily and mind-lessly shoved down and drowned in hot tea and diet cola. It's a part of my day as natural and second nature as brushing my teeth, going to work, feeding the cat and doing household chores. Binging and purging are on the same level in my life as other everyday activities. You don't have to think too hard in order to brush your teeth, it's a part of your day and you just do it. I can become so sure throwing up is a normal, commonplace behavior it seems like it isn't even a big deal to talk about it to others. I talk to other bulimics about it like it's a normal part of eating. "Rice is terrible, coffee tastes gross on the way up, ice cream tastes just as nice on the way up as it does on the way down."

It seems so normal to me that I have occasionally slipped or nearly slipped in mid-conversation and slurred out the truth, little bits of too much information, little behaviors only other bulimics would know about. I think about it so much that I see it in so many people, even if they most probably don't have an eating disorder. Everything relates to bulimia. I once even thought it was perfectly normal and okay to ask a girl at work who I had barely spoken to before (at that point) if she was bulimic. I was quite surprised it had upset her but then it hit me that it was obviously crossing a line and extremely rude. I also once heard someone retching in public toilets and immediately assumed the lady inside must be bulimic. I slipped a message with my email address under the toilet door. "I've been bulimic for x years. I know what you're going through. Email me."

Going to the local grocery store I would spend too much money buying luxury cakes, biscuits, pizzas, ready meals, ice creams and diet colas. The cashiers would give me a look and sometimes make rude remarks like sarcastic and smirky, "Enjoy your cake," or "You're going to get so fat eating all of this." I never could quite build up the courage to say, "Not that it's any of your business but actually I'm going to puke it but thanks for the warning." The embarrassment of buying so much food was because of, not the shame of eating so much, but someone else thinking I eat so much and thinking that I might digest the food and the calories I clearly didn't need. I wanted to be sickly skinny as a statement of being sad, angry and not a part of the world I hated, but more like a walking dead person. I felt dead and empty on the inside and I wanted a skeletal body to reflect that. I still largely do but I'm semi-okay with being average.

Although most days I freak out, am terrified of gaining weight and I would still like to lose weight to be on the lower end or "safer side" of average.

If I'm being careful to try to get everything up, there's an order with the binge: fruit first, savory food, sweet food and copious amounts of ice cream. There's certain cutlery I use, bowls and plates, cups. I'm comforted by the familiarity and ritual of preparing for the binge. Then there's the purge. A big binge equals a big release. The release of purging for me is similar to the release of cutting. It's cathartic. There's a feeling of calm afterwards. I used to purge as a form of punishment. I would see how many times I could throw up in a day and how dizzy I could get just for the satisfaction that I was hurting myself and I deserved it. Depression came first. I use bulimia to cope with the depression. Bulimia takes away the emptiness, numbness and frustration of depression.

There are times when acceptance of bulimia turns to hatred, times when it gets in the way of my semi-life, times when it reduces me to a zombie-like stupor. I hate spending my savings on food, when it's just going to be wasted in a couple of days. I hate eating food I don't even like the taste of when there's nothing else, or scouring through the cupboards trying to put something somewhat edible together. I hate the post-binge panics of having thousands of calories churning inside, waddling to the toilet hunched over in pain with my grossly distended stomach. I hate the difficult purges where I gag and heave and tear at my throat and see little swirls of blood in the vomit. At most I'll stop for a short while. At which point, my gag reflex would have returned, making purging easier and I'll be sucked into doing it multiple times a week or even several times a day, again.

The lowest point bulimia has reduced me to, as a vegetarian, is to completely abandon my morals and eat all kinds of meat with no restraint. My voracious bulimia-induced hunger would have me reaching for beef lasagna, Lorraine quiches, ham and mustard sandwiches, fish fingers and non-vegetarian candy. For now, it is not a problem to be a vegetarian, abstaining from meat, fish, gelatin and rennet. My consumption of animal products can still be an embarrassment to me. The amount of dairy ice cream and milk I can get through in a week, when I am in my bulimic phases, is utterly shameful.

For me, there's also another shame to this disorder. As a teenager, I would hide containers of vomit in various places in my room, under the bed, in the closet and locked in my desk. My sloppy teenage laziness and grubbiness, before I discovered the ease of disposing waste in the toilet, would mean the containers of vomit were left in my room for days and even weeks. I would go on a gruesome cleaning spree and find up to several inches of mold growing on the vomit. There was a time no one could enter my room or would even want to venture anywhere near it. The stench of putrid puke and rotting leftovers was unbearable and wafted outside my room. I lived like this because in my disordered state it was comfortable enough and I wasn't bothered to clean up. I was only bothered to open a window every now and then. I would rather have binged and purged again or wallowed in my teenage misery and anxiety listening to heavy metal music than to have wasted time cleaning.

Recently I have been trying very hard to eat healthily and not throw up. I'll have breakfast and rush out of the house. My current breakfast is porridge made with water, a banana and nuts or I'll have wholewheat toast with peanut butter and a banana. Lunch is usually couscous with vegetables, a sandwich or a jacket potato with salad. Dinner, however, is a harder challenge for me. A healthy meal at home, no matter how well balanced or filling, is a trigger for a binge. The problem is I don't want to stop eating; I'm still empty and unsatisfied. I can have six healthy, balanced meals a day, high fiber, high in unsaturated fat, with no dietary restrictions whatsoever and even exceed my nutritional intake but still will find stopping eating a gargantuan task.

Stopping eating once I start is on a par with holding my breath, like I'm delaying the inevitable. This is how it is sometimes easier to fast for the whole day rather than eat at least a little something to keep me going. Whether I fast or eat regular meals, obsessive thinking about food can make me look forward to my next meal so much I sometimes plan what I'm going to have. My mind will replay a long list of food, "pastries from the bakery, cakes and biscuits from the supermarket, get the ice cream from the store closer to home so it won't melt by the time I get it home." Then I'll go through the order the food will be eaten, where I'll sit in the house, what I'll watch on television while binging, when I can take breaks to purge.

It is easy to get lost in this obsessive thinking. Of course it is selfish and shallow, especially after watching the news for a bit of reality on what really needs to be worried about: wars, hate crimes, conflicts, missing children, abused children, suicides. I think, for me, bulimia has a similar effect as the "restricted behavior patterns" with autism. This focus of the mind on to seemingly insignificant details can wipe away everything else. As much as people can try to convince you to give up your unhealthy obsessions, nothing else exists for the short amount of time you are obsessing over something. Nothing else, I have found, can even replace them.

I don't have much hope of fully recovering from this in the future. This has been in my life for eight years; eight years of being a healthy weight, or overweight and therefore "you can't possibly have an eating disorder." I have all the hope in the world though of not letting this control my life like it used to. Bulimia has kept me wrapped in a cocoon, tainting my last few years of school, my college years and my early twenties and I will never let bulimia get in the way of my goals ever again.

Private therapy has mostly failed for me. A series of prescription medications has only fractionally alleviated the urge to purge (although it has helped a lot with depression). Getting through by myself and with my mountain of self-help books has failed. As desperate as I can become to get rid of this, in truth I am terrified of living without these behaviors. And now it's becoming increasingly easier to get rid of the food, just by bending over, no hands, it's too easy to stop. More importantly, I don't want to recover completely. I want to hold on to just a little bit of this disorder. I'm okay, perfectly fine like this.

10

Diagnostic Labels and Sexual Abuse

I spent three years starving before I discovered the joys, and inevitable pains, of binging and purging. I was already fucked up with food, as in I was scared to death of it. I had already lost most of my self-esteem, personality and ambition to succeed in any part of life that didn't involve calories, weight or food. What else did I really have left to lose? Apparently, oh so very much more.

It's really amazing to me, looking back on my behaviors and my way of thinking. I was depressed, I was overwhelmed with life, I couldn't cope with what was happening and what had happened to me when I was little and, yes, I am alluding to sexual abuse. Although it's taken me approximately 15 years to actually mention this, it is probably a reason, if not the reason, I'm so "messed up." I've collected quite a number of diagnoses over the years: anorexia, bulimia, eating disorder not otherwise specified (basically they're not really sure what the hell to label what you're doing), borderline personality disorder (BPD, mainly because I self-harm and am a bit more on the rebellious side when I'm in hospitals and many practitioners slap the BPD label, in other words "hard to treat" on me), post-traumatic stress disorder and major depression. Labels are nothing more than a way for clinicians to group people together based on like symptoms. I have issues, enough said.

I'm getting off topic, yes, bulimia is the subject. Bulimia is my best friend and my worst enemy. Nothing else on this earth is able to shut off my brain as well as bulimia. It all begins with restricting. I restrict my food all day long, because I'm scared of calories staying in me. It gets difficult throwing up at work or school all day. Throughout the day I plan, scheme and dream of what food I'm going to get, where I'm going to get it out and when I get to eat it. I like it the best when I have an unplanned night and I'm able to curl up in front of the television with my food and eat until I can't eat anymore. Then I get up, puke until I feel that it's gone and go back to the television. I repeat the following steps until I'm exhausted or until I run out of food. It has gotten to the point when I was actually angry when people called me at night. I was angry when people wanted to come over to my house or do something with me, and yes I have the audacity to wonder why it is I have no friends or boyfriends.

So the question I bet you are all itching to ask is, "Why do it? Why do it if it causes so much pain?" I wish I could answer that. I've been in some sort of treatment (be it therapy, inpatient, residential, day treatment) since I was 16 years old. I've spent six years fighting, crying, dying, surviving and here I am puking multiple times a week, which, to be honest, is progress. It used to be multiple times per day. It used to be so much worse, but it still sucks. If it took me six years to get this far, it's going to take me 60 years to be "better," whatever that is exactly.

Bulimia has ruined my life. Is it the bulimia or was it the abuse that's the cause? Maybe I like to say it's the bulimia because then I feel like I'm in control over my life versus saying that it's all *his* fault? I constantly lie to myself and others to make myself feel better. I want to lie while writing this. I want to say, "Bulimia ruined my life, but now with hard work and great treatment, I've reclaimed my life. I'm doing all of the things I never thought I would do. I'm finishing up college, I'm in a relationship with a man I love and my life is coming together." Oh how I wish I could say those things. They're lies though. My life *is* better than it was six months ago, a year ago, two years ago, but it still isn't where I want it to be.

It's been brought to my attention too many times that I am a black-and-white thinker and to those who don't speak therapist talk this means I tend to think in extremes, "all or nothing," "good or bad," "fat or thin," I have a hard time seeing the middle ground or "shades of gray." I get down on myself that my life still sucks and discount all the strides I've made. My life truly isn't as bad as I sometimes make it out to be and yet I'm not nearly as healthy with food as I sometimes suggest. It's a struggle. It's a daily, hourly, minute-by-minute struggle. My mind changes second to second. I'm a contradiction, mainly because I'm always changing my views, always fighting within myself. I'm struggling with the tenses in writing this. I'm aware I'm going from the present to past verbiage, but I'm not sure which one is correct. Some parts were the past, some are the present; some parts were present last week and now the past, although it could be the present next week. It's exhausting living in my head.

Shut up. I can think it all to death. I can talk about my eating disorder forever. I've analyzed, understood, picked apart, questioned every aspect of it. I know what functions it plays in my life and I know why I have an eating disorder. All of this information is fine, but it doesn't make me stop acting on my behaviors.

I have many deep, dark secrets about my sexual abuse I have not uttered to a single, living soul. In my head I can intellectualize that it's not my fault and that I was a little girl, but in my heart I still feel dirty. I think the healing process is to truly know in my heart it wasn't my fault and have compassion for the little girl I was and the woman I am now. If I know that, I won't need to punish myself for what happened then, punish myself for allowing my dad to sexually abuse me. I didn't allow him to do anything, I was five years old and he was my dad. If I intellectualize it, maybe it will sink into my heart.

It's tricky, trying to balance everything. I'm working in therapy on the sexual abuse and then sliding down headfirst into the depths of the bulimia because I can't deal with working on the sexual abuse. Retelling my story and feeling those things I felt when I was little make me want to puke, make me want to hurt and make me want to rip off all of my skin and die. (Yes that is extreme, I admit the border-line diagnosis probably isn't completely off-base.) I slide back into the bulimia hardcore and my therapist backs away because she's scared.

Bulimia is my safety net and my destruction. I don't know if I can survive in this world without having my crutch and I don't know how much longer I can survive in this world with my crutch because it is slowly killing me. I love and hate my eating disorder. I love that it shuts off my head, my thoughts. I can spend a night binging and purging instead of crying over what happened to me. I can obsess over the scale instead of going out on dates and having flashbacks when they kiss me. Right now, bulimia is still my friend, sometimes more of a best friend and sometimes more of an acquaintance. I call on her when I need comfort, safety and protection, although I'm trying more and more to call on people and live my life without my disease or crutch.

I'm going to end this with hope. Eventually I will not need my crutch. I will be secure enough in myself, in my body, in my mind and my abilities to survive and self-soothe. I will not need to rely on a self-destructive disease to live. I need to have this hope to keep on going, to keep on fighting; fighting for the life my dad took from me and fighting for the life bulimia is stealing from me. I will prevail, goddammit.

11

College plus Eating Disorder Equals...

One of the stereotypes about college is the Freshman-15 phenomenon. When introduced to the copious amounts of food at their college dining halls, first-year students tend to run wild without abandon. But it wasn't the buffet-style dining halls or the famous fast food chain in the student center that led me to bulimia. What led me to bulimia were the frat parties, loud and dark and filled with newly independent teenagers. Frat (short for "fraternity') parties were a great place to dance and drink (and drink and drink and drink) and maybe have a little fun. By the first few weeks of my freshman year, I would be going to these parties multiple times in one weekend. Already anorexic, I would latch on to purging as an outlet for my little drunk body. I would be coming home from another party, drunk off whatever the frat boys put in their jungle juice and I would remember how sick I would be in the morning. The ever-present hangover was my worst nightmare. I had an eating disorder for five years, but would never purge. Do you remember being young and having the stomach flu?

Throwing up would always make my five-year-old self feel better. My oft-intoxicated 18-year-old self realized the same principle must hold true to avoid the painful nausea of a hangover. Thus, coming back to my dorm after a night out I could usually be found sticking my fingers down my throat in our communal bathrooms. Still dizzy and giggly with a buzz, I'd let out a chuckle at the colors appearing in the toilet bowl, blue, green, red. It would be an abstract painting and it would soothe me. The soothing quality of ridding my body of alcohol soon became addictive and terrifying. Soon, I was purging every time alcohol hit my lips and because I was 18 and independent, alcohol would hit my lips at least three times a week. I quickly realized that if I could purge alcohol so easily, maybe I could purge the very little food I was eating.

This realization three years ago would dangerously alter my life. I was at college for maybe a month when I started purging. I wouldn't blame my fast descent into bulimia on my college experience. I would say college helped that descent along a little. I was free, from my parents (overbearing), friends (worried) and the good girl image I clung to in high school. College was a time for me to try new things and that is exactly what I did. Unfortunately those new things didn't include joining the Jewish community of my college or trying out for the crew team. Those new things included puking what I drank and ultimately what I ate. I'm in my senior year now and I've grown in many ways throughout my years in college. I'm no longer a drunken freshman. However, the habits I developed those first couple of months at college still remain with me. I sometimes worry the only information I learned at college was how to vomit what I'd eaten. I may earn my diploma, I may have spent four and a half years sitting in cramped lecture halls with 200 other students, but I will have spent these years picking at a plate of salad or crouched over a toilet bowl.

12

Not Good Enough

It is difficult for me to remember a time when I was satisfied with my body and not concerned with what I ate or how I looked. I remember being about six years old, standing nude on the bathroom counter so I could examine my body in the mirror. I was an average-sized kid, neither skinny nor fat, but I was always afraid I'd get fat someday. I wanted to be skinny. I wanted to be like the rail-thin girls I knew who seemed so effortlessly tiny. I wasn't. My body simply wasn't made that way, but I wanted it to be and if I had known how to get that way, I probably would have tried.

My mother was always dieting, always dissatisfied with her weight. This was in the late 1980s and early 1990s when low fat was the big thing, so my mother counted fat grams. I did too. Every morning, I would eat my cereal while I read the nutrition label to see what was in it. I realized at some point that protein was good and sugar was not, so I would look to see how much protein and sugar were in different foods. This meant nothing to me at the time since I hadn't yet connected the dots that what I ate affected my body shape and size. It just seemed to be a good thing to do, so I did it. I did my mother's aerobic exercise tapes too, hoping this would ensure I would look like the spandex-clad women on the tapes when I was older and would never be fat.

But while I read labels and bounced around the living room in imitation of the aerobics instructors, I also ate. I would sneak into the kitchen when everyone else was busy, grab cookies or bread or whatever I could get quickly and quietly, stuff it into my pockets and run upstairs to eat it before anyone saw me. If I were to get caught, I would be in trouble. My family had eight kids and no money. Food, especially treats, was limited. Not in the sense that we didn't have enough, we did, but we were absolutely forbidden to eat anything without permission. As far as I remember, my early days of binge eating weren't related to emotions or anything like that. I just liked to eat and I liked the thrill of getting away with something.

Then again, there were undeniable emotional issues. No one knew, but they were there. I was extremely sensitive as a child, my feelings were hurt easily. I was (and still am) embarrassed by the slightest thing and any criticism stung for weeks. I took everything personally and every mistake or correction was interpreted as a personal failure, proof that I was hopeless and would never be good enough. I wanted to be good enough. I wanted my parents' approval. I wanted them to be proud of me. I could never get this from them, my personality was not what they wanted. I have one older brother who is the stereotypical oldest child: compliant, neat, successful and so on. I was impulsive, defiant, messy, disorganized and hyper-emotional. To my parents, this meant I was a lazy, selfish, sloppy, attention-seeking brat and I was told so over and over until I believed it.

Fast forward to age 11 and a few items of potential significance. One, I began the early stages of puberty and the binge eating I had been doing started to catch up on me. I had always been active, so I had never been overweight, but my body was starting to mature and I was gaining weight. I still was not overweight. A little on the heavy side, perhaps, but looking back, it wasn't any more than normal. I didn't know this. I didn't know weight gain was normal around this age and that there was a reason for it. I thought I was getting fat. My worse nightmare was finally coming true and I was going to be fat like my mother.

Two, I got a paper route. I had money of my own and my route took me right by a grocery store. Translation: I could eat whatever I wanted, bought with my own money, and no one could stop me.

Three, I learned what eating disorders were and became obsessed. I wanted one. I wanted, specifically, to be anorexic. This would serve several purposes. Anorexia would make me thin and therefore perfect and therefore happy. It would show my parents I was unhappy and punish them for being mean to me. It would also possibly kill me. This is when I started to "diet." Dieting, to me, basically meant no desserts or snacks. Every Sunday morning, I would start a new diet. I would have a small bowl of cereal (never sugary stuff) and a small glass of juice. Naturally, by the time lunch rolled around, five hours later, I was famished. So I would generally screw up the "diet" and have to start again the next day. I never lost any weight doing this, but I kept trying.

I also started reading about dieting at this time. I read my mother's magazines and I would look to see what the latest diet advice was, what foods were good and what was bad, how much exercise I should be doing. Occasionally there would be an article about eating disorders and I would read it over and over.

I found a book as well, about eating disorders and other problems common in elite gymnasts and figure skaters. This is where I got the idea to throw up what I ate. It seemed perfect. I could eat and still lose weight. So I set out to make myself throw up. I couldn't do it. I tried and tried and couldn't figure it out. I couldn't do it until I was 16. In the meantime, I stayed in the same cycle of alternately trying to restrict my food intake, then getting too hungry and binging and my weight continued to increase until I actually was overweight.

When I was 14, I was unquestionably heavy. And when I was 14, I started ninth grade at a public high school after being home schooled my entire life. I was completely unprepared. It was a culture shock. I had no idea where I fit in. I was surrounded by thin, pretty girls who embodied everything I thought I should be. I had a couple of friends I knew from church, but otherwise I didn't know anyone. I didn't dress right, I didn't watch the right television shows, I didn't listen to the right music. I was a total misfit. My basic personality didn't help, I had long ago realized if I couldn't be quiet and pretty and perfect, I'd be funny. So I was. I was loud and hyper and very impulsive and I hated this. It had worked well enough when I was younger, but all of a sudden, no one thought I was funny anymore. I quite literally did not know what to do with myself.

I hated myself. I hated that I couldn't seem to be who I wanted to be and the depression that had been a part of my life since childhood started to grow and spread. At 15, I started cutting myself as a way to take the edge off. Cutting numbed me. Self-harm calmed my raging emotions and somehow made everything seem okay.

Near the end of my sophomore year, I had a physical and found out I weighed 159 pounds. I was five feet and three inches. I stopped eating and started taking laxatives and diuretics (since I still could not induce vomiting, I figured this was the next best thing). I started running, in preparation for soccer tryouts that August. I lost about 20 pounds that summer and made the soccer team. The amount of exercise I was getting at practices, the lack of food (I was still binging, but was eating so little in between that I still lost weight) and the hugely triggering effect of the thin, wiry bodies of some of my teammates took another ten pounds off that fall.

I had to take health that year. As part of the course I watched a movie about two friends with eating disorders. I loved it. It fascinated me. I distinctly remember the other girls in the class talking about the main characters, saying they were too thin and looked "gross." I couldn't see what they were talking about, the girls in the movie looked perfect to me. Never mind that one of them died in the end – I wanted to be like that.

It was around this time I finally figured out the trick to throwing up. I remember this clearly, it was a Wednesday night in February of 2000 (the twelfth, I think). I threw up macaroni and cheese in the bathroom sink, not the toilet. I didn't want to take the chance of "splashback." That night at church, I wrote in my journal about how I had finally done it. I was ridiculously excited about this. I told myself I wasn't going to let it get out of control, I would keep restricting, but if I happened to eat too much or was in a situation where I couldn't get out of eating, I would throw up. It was supposed to be a back-up plan.

By the end of the school year, I was throwing up at school almost every day. After school, I would go home, eat and eat, then throw up again and would sometimes do so after dinner, too. My parents eventually found out about it and about the cutting. They were, predictably, angry at me. They assumed the cutting was for attention (which is why I hid it for a year?) and never thought I was actually throwing up. They believed I was making it all up, again, for attention. I didn't want attention like I did when I was little, though. I wanted to disappear. I wanted to live in my own little world and not be bothered. At the same time, I was afraid of being invisible. I didn't want to be ignored. I wanted someone to notice that things were not okay and to take my problems seriously. I wanted someone to do something, to fix the mess I had gotten myself into. I was completely out of control and didn't know how to stop myself. So I stopped trying.

Once again, I was not good enough. I wasn't thin enough, I wasn't pretty enough, I wasn't neat enough, quiet enough, smart enough and now, I wasn't even sick enough. At this point, I had basically given up. I decided if no one was going to try to stop me, then I just wouldn't stop. I binged and purged whenever I could, I went weeks on less than 500 calories a day, I cut daily, I attempted suicide a few times and then what? Now what? I wish I had a happy ending to this story, but I don't.

My last year of high school was seven years ago. In the past seven years, I was hospitalized twice, dropped out of high school, got kicked out of college, joined the military, got married, had a baby, gained weight, lost weight, got out of the military, went back to college, made a few friends and learned to drive. Not in that order. It hasn't all been bad. I've had some good times, met some great people and learned a lot along the way. But at the end of the day, I am still not good enough. My house is not clean enough, my grades aren't high enough, my son isn't obedient enough. I am not thin enough. I am obviously not good enough for my husband. If I were, then he wouldn't cheat on me.

I am still bulimic. Very few people know. My husband and family are all clueless but a few close friends found out unexpectedly last winter. We talked about it at first, they tried to help, but I have stopped talking. I wonder sometimes if I will ever stop. I want to, at times. I don't want to live the rest of my life like this. I have screwed up so much, so irreparably, largely due to the eating disorder. I hate that. I hate what my life has become and what it will be. At the same time, I am afraid that if I let go, I will never be thin, and then I will never be perfect, and then I will never be happy.

I am afraid to let anyone know what's really going on. I'm afraid, mostly, of people's reactions. I don't want anyone else to see me how I see myself. I'm still not sick enough. I still don't have a "real" problem. I'm a fat girl who knows how to puke, but I'm not skinny, so I can't have a legitimate eating disorder. I'm afraid I won't be taken seriously or that people will think I want attention or that I'm being dramatic. Someday I'll be thin enough and then I can stop. Not yet. But someday, when I am skinny, when I am perfect, when I'm good enough to deserve help. Just not yet.

13

An Addictive Personality, Food and Alcohol

I have just finished my lunch. I had a chunk of fresh baguette with cold chicken, crème fraîche, spinach, spring onion and tomato. After, I had a bar of chocolate. Something new, I saw it in the supermarket when I went for the bread this morning. All very nice, all very different to any day you'd care to name between this time 4 to 18 years ago. From late summer/early autumn 1989 to the same time in 2003, I rarely ate a normal meal or had a normal visit to the grocery store. If I ate at all, I'd make myself vomit after. If I ate it was either a fifth of this amount or this amount multiplied by – a great deal: a few whole baguettes, maybe, much of a chicken, a whole tub of mayo, several bars of chocolate, copious amounts of cola to wash it down and soften it up.

I'm 33 years old now and as you may gather from the above, for it is a typical lunch these days, I am in recovery. I have suffered with eating disorders for 14 years, from age 15 to 29. Nothing ever goes as planned in life and I certainly never planned to be a dirty, disgusting, wasteful, fat bulimic. Neither did I plan to be an abstemious, pure, good, clean, skeletal anorexic either, not really, but that's kind of beside the point. By the time I was able to judge anorexia/anorexics and bulimia/bulimics, they are precisely the terms I was using.

Back then is very different to now, I knew nobody in real life with an eating disorder. There was the story of a friend of my mother's grown-up friend who had chronic anorexia and had adopted two children; the one of a girl younger than me at school apparently hospitalized and made to eat porridge with cream. I knew nobody myself, much less had spoken to anyone or seen one. My first exposure was therefore literature. I borrowed a book, at 15, from the library. It was about a young ballet dancer who developed anorexia. She made me feel fat, like an inelegant elephant, enormous, disgusting and greedy. She weighed herself and so did I. She was American and I quickly became just as adept at working it out in pounds rather than stones.

I became very unhappy. I knew I was "chubby." I was, I know now, a "user" of food anyway. Nobody knew how much I ate. Possibly today that earlier part of my life would have been slapped with a diagnosis too, for it is surely not normal for a 13-year-old girl to sneak out of bed and cook a plate of oven chips in the night and eat them secretly, with the family asleep upstairs? This happened fairly frequently and it is not surprising then that the girl who was an unhealthy, picky eater at age four or five (chips and crisps were on the list, most other things no) became disordered in more ways than one by adolescence. At 15 I weighed 11 stone, 154 pounds, at five feet and four inches, I found. I was shocked, horrified, disgusted and, after a trip to the doctor about a chesty cough during which he made a harsh, cruel comment about my size, fat and at a weight which resulted in my locking myself in my room for hours, crying and sobbing, vowing to do something about it.

I was nothing but determined. I made up my mind to fit into UK size 12 jeans again and left them where I could see them all the time. I told nobody I was dieting. I just became, so far as anyone could see, careful. I avoided chips. I didn't eat packets of biscuits after school. I started going swimming. I started reading teen magazines and looking at the pictures of the thin models. I got hold of a calorie counter and memorized it. I started cooking for myself and the weight fell off, without puking. From September to Christmas I was down to eight and a half stone, 120 pounds. I looked great. It was the first time I'd bought a pretty dress for the season. People said I was like a different person, but I knew I had a way to go. How far? Well, there was no answer there.

I have an addictive personality. I didn't know it then but I soon found out and am still learning how to handle it. I knew then that nobody was going to stop me from doing this stuff that was making me feel good about myself for the first time in my whole life. I had been unhappy at school, bullied much of the time, teased for being chubby and intelligent, boring and "straight-laced." I felt very stupid at home next to my genius older brother who had a scholarship to a prestigious boarding school. I didn't fit in anywhere. I didn't want to hang around with boys and I didn't think the boys would think I was anything other than an unattractive fat girl to laugh at. But when I became thinner, people did look and they seemed concerned, even envious. The power felt amazing. I had never, ever had these beautiful girls look enviously at me for anything. I could do something, effortlessly was how it felt, that they talked and talked about. All they went on about was calisthenics, gym, recipes, fad diets. I just sat and listened, somewhat smugly. I could do something they wanted to but couldn't.

Those size 12 jeans eventually fit and then became too loose and then they made me look like a clown. By the time I was a size eight, February 1990, my mother snapped. I was sent to the doctor, asked a load of questions, weighed, referred to a psychiatrist and told I was suffering from anorexia nervosa. The only question I never liked answering was about purging. Ask me anything else and I'd tell you, but about puke and I'd clam up. I had made myself vomit, but not many times. I lost the weight initially by not eating. There was a very few times I snapped and ate too much and then made myself sick and I hated doing it. Worst of all, I felt so ashamed. I had liked being able to refuse food, deny myself. To eat it and then undo the damage, well, it felt out of control and dangerous and dirty. I felt like a bad anorexic. I liked being anorexic, valued it, didn't want to lose it. I felt like I did at last have an identity, people could see that I was unhappy. It was no longer all hidden inside. So, for the first two years or so, I tried my best not to vomit.

But I lost too much weight. The result was my appetite exploded. I'd stabilized around six and a half stone, 91 pounds, for a while, but then panicked that I was still fat and stepped up my efforts and went down to five stone, 70 pounds. From there, it felt like something snapped. For the first time, I was drawn to sweet, calorie-rich food, especially chocolate, and I binged on it. I would binge on it every day, methodically. I didn't have the space or time (I was at sixth form college, age 18 and living at home) to be wild and crazy, to stuff my face with whatever. Neither did I have the money to go crazy. I felt crazy though, I felt like I needed to eat and eat and eat, it was like a chemical reaction in me that suddenly snapped and suddenly screamed. All the money I'd saved over the last few years dwindled away as I developed a 600g to 800g chocolate habit. I managed to block the kitchen sink with solidified fat. I usually puked into bowls that I hid in the wardrobe. As time went on and ice cream became part of my daily binging, the two liter tubs were very useful, since they could be cleaned out and reused. Chocolate, especially my chosen kind, 79p for 200g of misshapen ones, were pretty easy to get back up as there were soft centers in them that made the chocolate softer overall. The boxes were small, so I could carry two or three in my school bag and my mother would not notice. The sweets were unwrapped inside, so it was quick and easy to get through them, and I don't know, but my brain just loved the sugar rush.

As time went by and opportunity came my way, I expanded my binges to whatever I could steal from the house that wouldn't be easily missed. Bowls of cereal were a favorite, sometimes biscuits and ice cream or toast. I rarely had the place to myself, so binging and purging was behind my bedroom door. Whenever I had more than a minute or two in an empty house I was up the stairs to puke or dispose of some of the liters of puke in the closet. It did smell, of course, especially when whatever was in there fermented and bubbled over the edge of the box, milk being especially bad and smelly. My mother did suspect eventually, but generally I was the only person who'd go in there. And I didn't care about the smell. Occupational hazard, I guess. As long as I wasn't gaining weight, I could deal with all the crap.

During this time, I was in treatment. But never, ever did I go with the wish, intent and hope to get well. It was to get my family off my back, nothing more and nothing less. I didn't want to give up my eating disorder. I didn't want to stop being thin. I didn't want to stop the bulimic side of it all, either, though that was the part I was most ashamed of. I was never ashamed of having anorexia, but the waste and disgust of vomiting food, the out of controlness of binging, the pain and discomfort of laxatives, which I sometimes used, but not too much as I was afraid of destroying my bowel. I never admitted to any of it at the time. My behavior therapist thought she was being very observant one day and had caught me out when she pointed out the scabs on my knuckles she assumed were from putting my hands in my mouth to be sick. I was most offended by that and denied it completely. Actually, she was wrong, as I'd quickly become hands-free and rarely have ever used my fingers to purge. But she was right in a way – yet still I denied it.

Eventually, as I finished my A levels, I was forced to go into hospital, a four-week experience that just reinforced how utterly inadequate a non-specialist psychiatric unit is for someone with an eating disorder. It started off okay, with them monitoring me after each meal, but by week two I was able to slip off the ward alone, go to the visitors' shop and buy chocolate and biscuits and cola, which I took up to my room, hid and binged and purged at night. I was never caught and felt nothing but contempt for the staff. That I was sabotaging my treatment, such as it was, didn't bother me one iota, as I'd only gone there to get my family off my back anyway. It turned out to be the last time, for a long time anyway, that I did anything like that to please them, as when I went to college, emotionally speaking, I was on my own.

I discharged myself from the hospital after a month, against medical advice, but as the doctors could find nothing unstable enough to section me with, off I went. It was to be the end of any treatment for another ten years. That October, I went off to college and thus followed three very bleak years. It makes me sad to remember for, although I technically succeeded and achieved a 2:1 honors degree, my main memory is of the day-to-day grind of being a full-time bulimic. I was still underweight and I suppose would have been diagnosed anorexic, but I never ever restricted, I just vomited everything I ate. Every single day, many times each day, I was stuck in this cycle of buying food, eating it, purging it and then disposing of it. I fitted my studies around my full-time job of bulimia. A typical day would see me up at 10 am for a lecture, off to the campus shops at 11 am to buy enough chocolate for the bus ride to town, find a toilet in town to purge, go to several grocery stores to buy cereal, bread, butter, jam, syrup, milk, chocolate and crisps, lug my bags home on the bus, spend up to three hours binging and purging with the television on, pass out for an hour or so, go back to the campus shop for more food, binge and purge for a few more hours. Then I would prepare a bowl of vegetables for dinner (the only thing I'd allow myself to be seen cooking in the communal kitchen as I didn't want to ruin the reputation I hoped I had), eat it, purge it, pass out again. I rarely did any work, rarely saw other people; I spent my life with food. During holidays at home with my parents, it was similar. I spent my days at the library, surreptitiously eating pounds of chocolate hidden in my jacket inside pocket. My evenings were spent in my room binging and purging the food I'd sneaked in. At home and college, I was lonely and miserable but I didn't know what to do about it. I wasn't prepared to try something different. I had few friends, no boyfriends, rarely went out to socialize. If anyone had asked, I'd have said, "I like my life just the way it is." I can see how sad that is in retrospect but at the time I was so locked in to myself that I truly believed it. It was just the way my life was. My choice to do the things I do.

What eventually broke that cycle was alcohol. A year after graduating from college, in 1996, age 22, I moved away from home again to start a diploma course in magazine journalism. Immediately, things were different. For the first time in my life, I was looking forward to something and made a conscious decision to try my hardest to eat better, to try to be healthy. I'd gained a little weight over the previous summer but rather than despise myself for it, I felt quite good, for the first time, somewhat attractive, even. I had some smart clothes, new contact lenses, my hair cut properly and, most importantly, I had hope. I had hope that life would finally start, that I'd have an idea of what I could spend my life doing.

I was to be living in a shared house, sharing with others from my new college, which, I thought, was a good thing, as I would not have, I hoped, the same chance to isolate and spend my life hiding away with food. And I was right, I didn't. This new course was very different from anything I'd done before. The other people socialized a lot at the end of the day and for the first time I went along and made some friends. I had occasionally drunk alcohol at college and always had too much and got drunk when I did, but it was so infrequent I didn't think anything of it and I never drank alone. I never even thought about drinking alcohol. I enjoyed alcohol. Alcohol made me feel even more like I was part of something, like I was finally able to connect with the people around me. With alcohol I could talk and laugh and communicate. I had energy and I felt like I was lit up from the inside. Not much wonder I loved it as much as I did.

And with my opportunities to be bulimic reduced, I simply substituted alcohol. For a while I had lofty plans about a new start, the reality was that I still had urges to binge and purge, I still desperately wanted time alone, to numb myself, to take the edge off life. But my new life was busy and full and I simply didn't have the time that bulimia demanded. So I started to drink where once I'd have binged and from the beginning I drank in a bulimic manner, an alcoholic, addicted manner. Drinking alone didn't concern me because I always binged and purged alone. Drinking in the street didn't bother me because I ate and puked in the street when I had to. All the things I had done that once might have disgusted me, before I was bulimic, I had done because I had to. When you are an addict you will do whatever it is you have to do. If I would have been told, "You'll puke in gutters in the street," "You'll hide liters of puke in your closet," "You'll block drains," "You'll spend thousands of pounds," "You'll steal money and food," well, I wouldn't have believed them. I would be horrified and disgusted. But I did all that and more. And so when I started to drink, I'd already done so much that was past my normal standards of behavior that I really didn't care too much. I am a person of high morals in general, but when I am feeding an addiction, all that goes out of the window.

14

Confession to My Roommate, A Day in My Life

Hey roommate, how's the studying going? Do you want to join me for a smoke break? Do you have a lighter? Thanks. How was your day? How did your Alcoholics Anonymous meeting go? Wow, 120 days, that's something to be really proud of. I'm so happy everything is working out for you.

How did my day go? It went well. I woke up, went to school, came home, did homework. So did your sponsor from home call you?

Actually, you know what? I haven't been honest with you and it's time for me to come clean. Every night, as we sit here smoking, you ask me what I did during the day. Every night, I lie to you. I always leave out the part of my day where I binge and purge my lunch and dinner.

I know you had no idea, which is exactly what I wanted. I'm always so scared you would notice. I go through great measures to keep it hidden from you and the other two roommates. You don't know this but I hide tons of junk food in my room and keep the healthy food in the pantry so I appear like a normal but cautious eater. Everyday on my way home from school, I stop by the nearest gas station to pick up chips, cookies and cakes. I stuff all my goodies in my backpack and run to my room. I'm sure you have noticed the days where I run right by you without acknowledging your hello. On those days I am afraid that if you were to look in my eyes, you would see my disease tucked away in my backpack.

I inhale the food without honoring its value of nourishment, energy and taste. I stuff all my insecurities of not being smart, thin, pretty and charismatic into my mouth and down my throat. Then like a lifeless zombie, my feet carry me to my toilet. I throw up all the food and the insecurities. It all collects in the toilet and I admire how I devoured and destroyed everything that made me feel horrible. I flush it all away and guess what? It is always the best part of my day. Why is something so messy, violent and sick the best part of my day? It's because it's the only moment of my day when I feel victorious over my life.

I've always wanted to tell you about the best part of my day. A part of me wishes I could say "Roommate, today was a great day. I threw up everything and I feel so much better." But instead I hide the candy wrappers under my bed and clean my toilet. When I come out of my room, I smile not because I'm happy to see you, I smile because I'm high off of binging, purging and successfully keeping the disease locked in my room.

How do I binge and purge? You really would like to know? First, you have to hate yourself, a lot. You have to hate absolutely everything about yourself, from the way you laugh to the freckles on your face. You have to hate yourself so much you will no longer have respect for who you are. When you no longer respect the person you were designed to be, you will not care if your body is nourished. When you no longer care for your body, you'll be numb to cram your stomach with cookies, chips and soda. You will not feel your stomach rip and stretch to fit the abnormal quantities of food packed into your stomach. You will not feel the pain of your nails scraping the back of your throat. The sting of vomit eroding your esophagus and mouth will never bother you if you can truly numb your body and suppress your feelings. The requirements do not end there. You also have to give up all your free time to devote to your new hobby. No longer can you enjoy being with friends and family, you can't study, you can't go to work, you can't go to school, you must stay at home and just binge and purge yourself to complete numbness. That's how you keep the walls around your heart sturdy and your emotions safe inside them. The bulimia will always keep you secure and numb. All you will ever need to worry about is keeping bulimia your secret.

If you are wondering how it started, it started my freshman year of college. I had just left an inpatient treatment center for anorexia and I was in a new city, in a new crowd and was given too much freedom. I began drinking and smoking weed that year. When my friends and I would drink or smoke, we would always get the munchies. We ate so much. I was appalled by how much I was eating, it had to go away so I learned to purge. It was an amazing feeling; being so high on a substance, eating so much and throwing it all up. All my friends gained weight and I stayed the same. I loved the secret and my secret stayed with me until now. This is why I am telling you this. It is the secret double life I live that seduces me to purge everyday. Exposing my secret takes its power away from me even if it is just a little bit. Telling you also solidifies my commitment to begin recovery. It's one thing to tell a paid therapist or a support group you are going to work at recovery, but it is completely different telling someone who is also working on recovery that you are joining them on the journey of self-recovery.

Please tell me, what is recovery like? What is it like to feel emotions come and go? What do you do with all your free time away from an addiction? When will I begin to feel real again? How much will recovery hurt? How hard will it be? Oh my gosh, what am I doing? I am going to need another cigarette. Do you still have that lighter?

15

Becoming Bankrupt and Losing Everything I Had

Five years ago I was standing in cap, gown, honor cords draped around my neck amidst other graduates, potential in the air, congratulations abounding. Today I stand in line for the food bank, amidst others whose lives have gone awry leaving them homeless, broke, lost, sick, depression laying its thick cloud overhead.

As many people who struggle with eating disorders, I was once that successful adolescent who had everything going for them, top 10 percent of their graduating class, varsity athlete, applying at Ivy League colleges, I was going to "go somewhere." My world began to slowly crumble even in high school as depression began to creep into my life with bouts of self-harm. My college years were interrupted with suicide attempts and self-harm that were so serious that I was going to the emergency room every week. It was after a near successful suicide attempt that led me to being kicked out of college when I decided to volunteer on a hospital ship that served the West Coast of Africa for six months; escaping the real world was always my way out.

The ship did change my life, I found myself for a little while and I also gained ten pounds since the ship was donating much of their food, thus the diet lacked balance. Always being athletic, I was never preoccupied with food or worried about my weight. However, when I came back and found I didn't fit into my clothes I did have a minor freak out. I lost half the weight just by being able to eat normally again, then decided to train for triathlons and lost the rest.

My first triathlon I placed in the top three. It was then, high on adrenaline and my first success in a long time, I decided that if I lost even more weight I would eat, come back and win next year. I would eat only 500 calories a day to do so. This went on for quite some time, but a body can only tolerate such a diet for so long. Thus, I discovered purging. If I ever went over 500 calories, up the food came. Oh how I curse that dreadful day. Soon the food started coming up naturally. This scared me, but not enough to stop. I just became sicker, as the disease became easier. I guess I was now what is known as "hands free." For anyone that tries to recover and is a "hands free purger" this just makes things more difficult.

From here my life becomes a series of hospitals, relapses, failed treatments, lost friends and one brief year of recovery. Any money I had left for my education went to hospitalizations so my diploma still lies empty. At the age of 25 I have had to declare bankruptcy because of all my medical bills. I will never be able to get a credit card, own my own house, or get a car because my credit has been ruined by overdrafting my account from buying binge food and letting medical bills go to collection.

Eating disorders truly do rob you of everything: friends, family, relationships, your self and they do become your only friend. I now live in small cell of public housing, the dormitory for the mentally and physically disabled. I go from food bank to food bank to get binge food. At first the dissonance at the food bank was what foods I could get that were on my meal plan. Now it is what I get that I can binge on and how much I can fit on my bike.

My social life is on the internet on eating disorder forums. My scrapbook is pictures of culinary creations I have concocted. I have lost all of my friends because of my eating disorder. They don't know how to relate, they don't know what to do with me and frankly, they're doing much more productive things with their lives.

Meanwhile, I'm living on the state system. I now qualify for disability because the disease has made me so sick. This gives me just enough money to pay rent each month, but not enough to pay my medical bills and get food. Thus, I'm led to steal to keep my disease alive. I have been caught stealing. I have been to jail. I face fines that I cannot pay. There are only so many times you can tell a judge "Bulimia made me do it" before they start losing compassion. I am scared, but I am so numb and disconnected from myself that I still indulge in the act anyway just to get the adrenaline. This is the conundrum of the disease.

State insurance itself is a joke. I go in to see the doctor and they don't even look at you. I have to have a physical exam despite what my complaint is. They just chalk it up to the eating disorder and leave it at that. If your labs come back abnormal you no longer get a phone call because they know you won't do anything about it, you're a "lifer." On top of that, you have to meet what's called a "spend down" every six months. Mine is currently over $1000. Explain to me how I'm supposed to pay that if I only get $800 a month. Thus, I go without medical care for over half a year or get sent to collections trying to get medical care in order to meet my "spend down" and get my coupon back.

I've been keeping a blog recently. I haven't had a car in over five years. I randomly zoom around town on my crappy bike, long gone my beautiful tri bike, having sold it for medical expenses, dodging in and out of cars, hopping a bus here and there when my anxiety is not too bad, dropping my discounted disability quarter for fare. People don't understand why it is so hard for me to make my appointments or how painful it is for me to lift my bike up onto the bus. It's difficult to get groceries to and from my housing. I get mistaken for a homeless person all the time because of what I wear. My brain has gotten so fuzzy lately I can't remember one day from the next.

This disease has taken everything from me. My family barely speaks to me, my bank account is in negative numbers and I duck every time a police car passes by. I pray for the heart attack that never comes, because like everyone with an eating disorder, I think I'm invincible. So why do we stay stuck here? What draws us in? Why can't we let go? As in my behavioral therapy classes, what keeps us from acting "opposite to the emotion?"

Fear. I don't know who I am anymore and I'm scared to find out.

16

I Want to Be Like You

Pretty, frail, young, beautiful, graceful, thin, astounding, shocking, perfectionist. These adjectives may be used to portray and describe people in the entertainment industry. Stars who suffer from the glamorous "thin disease," words used to describe females in films who have an eating disorder. I know the truth. I work in the entertainment world, I am female, I am young(ish) and I have been described as thin and pretty. People love me, they crave my attention, they want to be me, they want me in their photos, they cry when they have to say goodbye, basically I am adored. I frequently get comments such as "Wow, if I do a gym class, will I get your body?" "You are sooo good on stage," "I love your clothes/make up/hair/shoes," "I wish I had your dedication to go to the gym," "I want to be *you* when I grow up."

Well, ladies and gentlemen, you really want to be like me? I warn you, this is not some made-for-television movie, where everything comes up smelling of roses. This is my truth as someone who has suffered from self-harm, depression and eating disorders for the past 17 years of my life. It is bleak, dark, boring, lonely and horrific. You still want to ride? Jump in and fasten your seatbelts – the secret world of eating disorders.

First of all you have to clear your mind. Do it. Clear your mind of everything. You are no longer allowed to plan going out or stopping by a food outlet to grab a snack. Everything you think must revolve around food. Everything that passes your lips must be calculated: when you last ate, how much you ate, when you will eat again, what to buy in the supermarket, can you control yourself in the supermarket? Do you have time alone at home tonight to have a binge? Will anyone notice an entire cake missing? Where are you going to throw up, because the food can't stay inside you? That is bad, bad, bad, and against the rules.

Situation: corporate lunch, 12 people. People commenting on how little you are eating, how you are really pale. Small observation, conversation moves on. Your reality: I am eating really well. Small amounts, no need to throw up afterwards, but people kept making comments about how little I eat, which made me feel uncomfortable, because I am really trying and I didn't eat a lot less than everyone else, but for starters we had a lot of small dishes and they filled me up. I can't eat anymore because otherwise I will have to purge it up later. On the other hand, what if I eat loads and then carry on the binge at home? How much longer have we got here? When does the supermarket close? Do I have any soft bread left in the house? Maybe I can pick up a takeaway pizza, but I need to get some diet cola as well. What is going to be open at this hour on a Saturday? If I binge and purge tonight, tomorrow is Sunday, the gym is closed, I have work and I have to eat dinner in public. Well I can skip breakfast and lunch, just have dinner to compensate. Maybe if I get those soft chocolate chip buns, they go down well, ooh and some melted chocolate bars warmed up in the microwave. Oh no, will the supermarkets still be open? How much cash do I have on me? Maybe I'll just go to the petrol station instead, yeah and then I can get some donuts. Well, I might as well eat dessert here. No, I have to keep up my façade. Small meals, healthy eating, I have to be perfect.

Are you still there? To have this disorder, you have to be obsessed with food, it rules your life, you replay things said in your head a hundred times. You don't even realize you are thinking these things. These thoughts are just a normal constant dialogue going on 24/7 in your head. A normal dinner conversation must be kept up with, but internally you are constantly worrying and obsessing and it will take over.

Situation: you are invited to go ice skating after work with a group of friends. Your reality: Great. I'll go home and change and then I'll be right there. I have already eaten lunch, there is no food involved, I am feeling okay today, haven't thrown up for a couple of days. I can enjoy myself and be "normal."

Situation: afterward the skating people start getting hungry, so they decide to head over to a famous fast food outlet for a snack. Your reality: this poses a problem. I can't admit to being hungry, I have never, ever said out loud "I'm hungry." If I ever am hungry then I suppress the hunger until it is in my "plan" to eat. The people I am with just admitted to being hungry and decide to get some food. Logical, no? If you have an itch, you scratch. Why can't I do this? Such a regular thing to do, but which causes me great trouble. So, I am just going to go in there, sit with them and not order anything. Hopefully they won't notice. Everyone orders fatty forbidden foods. These foods are only allowed if it is part of a plan to binge and purge afterwards. Conversation turns to joking and diets, they begin saying how they would never do one because they love food too much. I know an eating disorder is not a diet. Diets are about losing a bit of weight, eating disorders are about trying to make your whole life better through food. I know this. I have been in therapy, so why can't I stop? I know that I just use food as a weapon/comforter/enemy/agony aunt as and when needed. I know deep down the problem I have is self-image. I hate the way I look and still believe if I weighed xx my life would be great (even though I know this isn't true). I have yo-yoed my weight forever and at the end of the day it's not about the food, it's about the feelings they are disguising. But uncovering those feelings is a long and painful process, so much easier to just go on day-by-day obsessing and fantasizing over food.

Are you still here? Bored yet with the thoughts? I hope you haven't forgotten these things have to play on a constant repeat/replay in your head. Anytime you go near food you hear words such as "You're a fat, pathetic failure," "You don't deserve to be happy," "Look at you, you disgusting pig, no one likes you." You have to be obsessing over food/weight to such a degree that not only is it the first thing you think of when you wake in the morning and the last thing you think of before you go to sleep, but it occupies your dreams too. I'm going to help you a bit to really "get into" being me. Imagine:

1. Never feeling you are good enough. Ever. At anything. Ever. At anything. Ever.

2. You have to isolate yourself from all your friends, because at the end of the day a social gathering poses potential problems. However, being at home alone you can eat and binge what the hell you want to, you can throw it all up again. You can repeat that all night if you want to.

3. Forget having any sort of relationship with anyone because your self-worth is so low you can't imagine anyone would possibly like you and you don't want to face up to inevitable rejection.

4. Now remove all your energy. The cross between not eating or binging and purging leaves you energy drained. When you are not working you are too tired to go for a walk, to climb the stairs, to meet friends.

5. You feel like a fraud the whole time. Once you maybe were happy and smiled. Now smiles are forced. Also, your teeth are pretty messed up from the acid coming up from your stomach so you don't really like to smile. However, it is part of your job and the show must go on. Is the smile real? Absolutely not. Inside there is nothing but a deep empty black hole.

Well, we are nearly done, not much more left to teach about being me. Of course, the inevitable must be explained – laxatives and vomiting. Mainly these are my bulimic drugs of choice.

Laxatives: given to people to aid constipation. Right? Wrong. These are a potential heaven for us bulimics, the (incorrect) belief that you can stuff yourself with laxatives therefore speeding up the disposal of all the thousands of calories you have consumed and it all comes out the other end. However, you have to be prepared. First, if the recommended dose is about two, then no less than 15 will do. Taken at night, they will kick in. You will be doubling over in pain, barely able to reach the toilet. Everything comes out in liquid form and it burns. So much pain you can't stand. You might as well sleep on the toilet. Sometimes you don't reach the toilet in time. Clothes, bedcovers and everything must be changed, the pain is still there. The pain is crippling. Worse than any period pain ever. Laxatives are bad news. Laxatives don't help you lose weight. Laxatives just mess up your large intestine and carry a whole lot of other bad health side-effects. Do I care? Not at all. The whole point of this is to harm ourselves, get rid of the bad food and inflict pain on ourselves. We are bad, fat, ugly people, and we deserve to be punished.

Binge and purge: eat, stick two fingers down your throat, food comes up. Right? Wrong. It doesn't happen like you see in the movies. First the binging process turns you into some kind of wild animal eating out of a trough. Multiple saucepans on the go at once, sweets, chocolate, crisps, muffins, stuffing them in your mouth faster than you can chew or swallow, food and tears screaming down your face, mouth stuffed full, all washed down with some nice diet cola. You carry on eating after you feel you are going to burst, because this takes away all the bad things in your life. Food represents all the treats you have denied yourself and all the bad things that have happened. Eat them and enjoy them, then throw them up and get rid of them. So, the kitchen is a mess, you cut your finger opening a can, but just carried on eating with the blood dripping. Nothing is more important at this moment than the food.

Off to the bathroom. The next hour is spent with your hand down your throat, slogging back diet cola, horrible noises, retching, puke everywhere: toilet, floor, carpet, clothes, hair, hands. Tears are still streaming down your face. You can barely breathe because your hand is permanently down your throat, maybe you even lick the toilet bowl to induce some more vomiting. Your hand is red sore, maybe some cuts on your finger, often blood vessels burst in your eye. Acid burns your oesophagus, throat, mouth and hand. After a while the smell makes your eyes water even more. Guess this wouldn't really make prime time viewing. Afterwards you do get this kind of "high" like floating on air, the world seems invincible. All is good in the world and in your life because you just binged and purged. Then you get back down to the reality of cleaning up.

So what makes me qualified to teach you all of this? I stopped eating when I was eight. People noticed and one lunchtime I was force fed in the dining room in front of 300 other kids. From then on I developed a fear of eating in public. However, to shut people up I started eating things and throwing up afterwards. That went on for ten years. This involved sometimes not eating, sometimes abusing laxatives, sometimes eating normally, sometimes throwing up everything I ate. Then I emigrated to paradise and to a certain extent the behaviors stopped. However, paradise soon became reality: it doesn't matter where I live, the problem is *me*, within myself. I am the one with all the self-doubt.

Now I live a relatively normal life. I can talk about my food issues, I know I have them, I have had therapy for god knows how many years. I mainly have it under control, but if something bad or stressful happens in my life, I turn to my safety blanket: bulimia. My head splits into two parts, the logical side which knows that binging is not the answer to my problems and the irrational side, which convinces me it is. I don't take laxatives any more, but I do overexercise to give myself "permission" to eat. For me, I can't really remember life without an eating disorder, so this eating disordered life has become my normal routine. I can't imagine not worrying about my weight, constantly monitoring what I eat, how much I work out, binging, purging. It is just all a part and parcel of who I am and, yes, sometimes I do get shocked that not everyone thinks and acts this way.

As mentioned I have had a lot of therapy: doctors, counsellors, psychiatrists, psychologists. We have dealt with a lot of hard stuff: family issues, depression, cutting myself, suicide, but have never really gotten to the bottom of my eating issues. I am a "lifer" as it were. Seventeen years of my life has been spent with this disorder and I can explain all about why I do it and how to control it until I am blue in the face, but I just can't stop it.

So, now ask yourself again: do you really want to be like me?

4

Sex, Lies and Hedonism

Hello. I would just like to start this out by giving you somewhat of an idea of who it is writing this. I am 26, attractive, alcohol addicted, eating disordered and neurotic as all hell. I have hobbies, friends, I can keep a job, and for the most part I have my head screwed on straight. Until it comes to myself, that is. I'm promiscuous, an attention whore when I'm not being an antisocial loner, anxious and completely preoccupied with my looks, although admittedly not in the way you would 'expect' an eating disordered individual to be. I'll get to that in a minute. I'm your classic ugly duckling, with a generous helping of poor coping skills and over-thinking mixed in and sprinkled with a somewhat out-of-character paranoid streak. Also, I am terribly arrogant.

So how did this all start? It's hard to say. I was a bookworm outcast when I was young and a depressed, unattractive teenager after that. I didn't realize it was so obvious, but it only took one incident of self-injury to get promptly tossed into the hospital and put on antidepressant

131

medication. From that point, the next few years saw me focusing entirely on my lack of a chest. I figured I'd get one eventually – everyone else did, after all – but it never happened. I felt unfeminine, unattractive and completely repulsive.

When I turned 18, I became an exotic dancer. Oh yes. I never got implants put in, not even after three and a half years of it. I had the appointment made at one point and I cancelled it. I was sitting alone having tea with myself, when it occurred to me how ridiculous that idea was. Surgery? Because, why? No matter what your body type, it will always be somebody's favorite and at this place in my life, I really felt it. So I kept my natural body, although the seeds were being planted. I was slowly becoming terrified of gaining any weight, for fear I would be chubby and breastless and even more mediocre looking than I currently deemed myself. Mediocre might be a nice way to put it. I had nightmares about my body. I was ashamed of it beyond words.

I failed to cover the promiscuity part. This may become important later for the big picture, so I should probably touch upon it somewhat. I lost my virginity at 13, quite willingly. Tossed it away, rather. I had a bit of a celibate break for a year or so, due to another round of antidepressant medication and spent up until quite recently sleeping around across three provinces. I did it because I liked sex, not so much because I wanted to feel needed or pretty or any of that mumbo-jumbo. No, this would be more due to my complete lack of impulse control. It's the same interesting little flaw that brought me to the ways of the bulimic and the alcoholic. Sex never made me feel pretty anyway, as

I was always sure I had the ugliest body of anyone that my many partners had previously seen naked.

I will never forget that meal. I had been starving myself for a little while at this point, one day literally deciding that I was going to starve myself. Not clear on how I came to such a conclusion. I can only imagine that it was months of stress with an emotionally abusive boyfriend, problems finding a place to live, having recently lost my job and dealing with over a decade of severe body hatred. It's like it all came to a head and all the stress needed to go somewhere and I made the decision to channel it into my eating. The meal, as it was, was seafood with my dad. It was delicious. I couldn't fake eating right in front of him and my conscience was bothering me too much to waste the food he was paying for anyway. So I ate it and thus got the first taste of heart-pounding, post-meal panic that would stick with me indefinitely. I did the only thing I would think to do and excused myself to go to the bathroom where I had my first purge. It was successful, right from the very first attempt. I remember walking back to the table feeling like I had just found a good, working solution to this whole starving nonsense.

I promptly dumped eight noticeable pounds off in the upcoming month. I felt so sneaky about the whole thing. I could eat and eat whatever I wanted, with none of the guilt. Naturally, I became more and more ravenous about it, the portions and desperation in it increased and I was starting to feel physical effects. I could purge up anything, donuts, sandwiches, Chinese food, entire cakes, pots of spaghetti, waffles, junk food, cookies, hamburgers, you name it. I insisted on speed-walking to my new job every morning and I allowed myself one small meal to digest a day. I spent my money on food and rehydrating drinks. I walked around weak and shaking and thinking constantly about eating, eating, eating.

At first I had a routine. I would eat 200 calories in the morning, jog my ass to work (in the middle of Canadian winter), eat one small meal in the day and have a good-sized binge and purge later at night. After a while, it started to slip out of my grasp. When stress in my life mounted, I'd mindlessly eat everything I could get my hands on. It was like all this crazy, neurotic energy would build up and I'd simply have to give it an outlet, so I did the only thing I could. I ate and ate and ate and vomited it all back up in the toilet. I'd stand back after, feeling relief of near orgasmic proportions. Maybe as you've guessed, I use sex much in the same way, but it is not so impromptu and tends to scare people less. Sex is healthy, overeating and vomiting cyclically is not, but they can still perform the same functions for you on occasion.

I had to stop smoking pot. I'd have paranoid panic attacks about what I was doing to my body and instead of fixing the eating issues, I simply cut that out of my life. This developed into a full blown anxiety disorder, which I have done massive work on correcting, but I still can't smoke weed anymore. I'm a little annoyed at having something I once enjoyed so ruined by something that became such a detrimental preoccupation.

I have learned to beat down anxiety attacks and I forced myself to control the binging, and subsequently, the purging. I do mess up from time to time, sometimes it is several times a day and sometimes I go for a couple months resisting the urge. In its place now is alcohol. I don't seem to be free of them both. When I spend a long stretch sober, I fall back into the old binging and purging cycles. When I am drinking all the time, I don't panic so much about my eating. I have no idea why, perhaps I numb myself?

There is, of course, a whole fun mental thing to all of this. This has remained constant throughout some very big changes in my life. Remember how I said I was an ugly duckling? I used to starve and want to lose weight to be pretty. Sometime in the last year, I've realized that I am pretty and now I'm horrified at that, instead. I used to puke up food when I felt fat and ugly, now I do it because I feel like I'm being stared at. Being lusted after irritates me and creeps me out. It could have something to do with not being used to it, I don't really know, but it sure is a trigger. I can't tell when someone actually likes me as a friend, as something more, or just wants to fuck me. I usually assume that they are not attracted to me until proven otherwise, which brings about results ranging from shame, paranoia and the feeling that people only look at me as a shell.

Hey. I spent a lot of time ugly. I had to develop other ways of getting attention from the ones I was attracted to. Whenever it hits me that the person I'm talking to is only interested in me on a physical level and not my brain or personality, it's a slap to the face that I have no words for. I feel invalidated, empty and useless.

18

The Lesbian
Bulimic Mafia

I can't remember the first time I purged. For many bulimics, a first "successful" purge is an experience as significant as a first kiss, something they can recount to the last detail. All I can say is that it happened at some point during my first term at college, when I was 18. I had been fairly overweight for much of my childhood and adolescence, but at the age of 15, I embarked upon something that began as a diet and culminated in severe anorexia. I also made a new friend when I was 16, someone I'd known of at school but had never really spoken to; that is until we were thrown together due to having chosen the same four A levels, notorious as the school anorexic.

As it turned out, she wasn't anorexic. Perhaps if she had been, my life would be different today. She was intelligent and funny, geeky in the good kind of way, similar to me on almost every count, and we quickly became great friends. She told me, after we'd been close for a couple of months, by which time my anorexia had already taken me firmly in its grasp, that she was bulimic. She'd suspected that I too was eating disordered and wanted to know for sure. I doubt it was a difficult deduction to make. At this point, I was surviving until dinner on coffee and chewing gum, which she could hardly have failed to notice, given that we sat together during lunch period, me drinking a diet cola while she consumed a meal which, to me, looked enormous. I had wondered, previously, how she managed to keep so trim a figure and eat the way she did. But all meals looked enormous to me by that time and I decided I must be imagining it. Of course, as it transpired, I was not imagining it and she was routinely purging the meal.

Soon, we became partners-in-crime. I would accompany her to the bathrooms after she'd eaten, keeping watch. If someone came in, I would cough loudly to draw her attention to their presence and operate the hand-drier to create some background noise. She, in turn, would support me in my insistences to other friends that I was "eating *plenty*, thank you very much." "What are you talking about? She had a sandwich today. I sat and watched her eat it." For the first time, I felt safe. In retrospect, it looks very much as if we must have been incredibly detrimental to each other's health, but it must be noted that we had each begun our unhealthy cycles of behavior independently. This was merely a support system; the knowledge that someone, at least, understood us and could comprehend that eating disordered people are not all ready to recover just yet.

We'd been best friends for almost two years when I left for college. I was bound up North and she had a place studying medicine at the (very respectable) local university. We were and, I suppose, still are stereotypical poster children for eating disorders: high-achieving, idiosyncratic, conscious of being constantly misunderstood.

Unlike many eating disordered people, though, we had been saved from utter loneliness. We had each other and there was no question of our losing touch because of the distance.

When I got to college, I had total control over what I ate for the first time in my life. To this day, I cannot recall why I decided it would be a good idea to eat as much as possible and then throw it up and to do this as a routine, binging and purging several times a day and subsisting on apples outside of this. I do know I began with ice cream, the friend to all bulimics. Sometime during that first term, I sent my friend a text message, "Well. It seems I have become bulimic." She said, "I'm sorry. Should I be? Are you all right?"

As far as I was concerned, after two years of anorexia, my newfound ability to eat anything I wanted and *lose weight* was more than all right. It was wonderful. I hadn't yet begun to experience thinning tooth enamel or stomach pain. Nor had I realized that, if ever I wanted to eat normally again, my digestive system would vehemently protest. I still felt, like a teenage smoker in the first thrill of the habit, that this was, almost, an indulgence, a pleasurable entertainment I could abandon at will. When I went home that Christmas, my friend and I proceeded to spend a month binging and purging together, at buffets and restaurants and at her parents' caravan. It was utter, utter bliss. I felt so grateful for my friend.

That first year at college, I lost an awful lot of weight, weight which seemed to fall off effortlessly, while the weight loss with anorexia had come at so great a cost that I had often felt that I would have committed suicide if it hadn't been for my friend. There had been dizziness and fatigue and always the tearing pain of hunger, which subsided at times into a dull ache, but which never completely disappeared. Bulimia was different. Bulimia allowed me to eat to my heart's content, provided I was prepared to spend the time purging and rinsing and purging again and still decrease in size at what was, to my parents' eyes, an alarming rate. I quickly learned to multitask. I would binge in my room in college while reading the necessary textbooks, while writing my essays, while proofreading, while doing anything. An inveterate planner, my hyper-organized mind wrapped itself gladly around the tightly controlled schedule that was my bulimia, calculating which route to take from the lecture hall back to college after my morning seminar in order to pass as many sandwich shops as possible or what to put into the oven first so it would be ready just as I was finishing with something else. I enjoyed and still enjoy it. When I went home for the holidays, my parents expressed increasing concern over my size, but I brushed it off, going out with my friend on great hedonistic adventures into the bulimic underworld. By this time, we were also regularly having sex, without being "in a relationship" beyond our friendship. We jokingly called ourselves the Lesbian Bulimic Mafia, LBM for short, and felt that nobody had ever been as close to us as we were to each other. Nobody else had ever really understood.

Midway through my second year at college, I fell in love with a girl in another part of the college halls who also read my subject. I, of course, told her nothing about my bulimia or my history of weight-related issues and the relationship became very serious, very quickly. At this point, I was still binging and purging in between and during my university work in the day, and seeing her in the evenings and at night and the two seemed to be working quite well. My previous girlfriend was happy for me. There had never been any suggestion that what the two of us had in that sense was anything other than casual sex, although there was a different sort of depth to it that derived, doubtless, from our long-established closeness and emotional intimacy. I loved my current girlfriend intensely, but I still loved food. It occurred to me for the first time when she invited me to stay with her and her parents during the long summer vacation that I was attached to my eating disorder in a very unhealthy way. Somehow, I had always managed to convince myself that it was an enjoyable thing: a lifestyle choice, almost. And yet here I was, now, in her home, knowing that I would have to eat like a "normal person," if such a thing exists, without purging and the idea terrified me.

Getting through the summer was very difficult. I have seen many people choose their eating disorders over the people they love and I am immensely glad I managed not to do this, but I can certainly understand why it is so often what happens. I was determined that my current girlfriend should not uncover my secret, but I also felt that I couldn't bring myself to stop, despite the fact that I knew it would hurt her if she found out. I felt guilty about that, certainly. Was I a bad person? Did I love my eating disorder more than I loved her? When she found out, she caught me purging on several occasions and I managed to convince her that it was something else until at last she told me firmly to give it up. Because she knew, I promised her, in panic, that I would stop doing it. She said I had better or she would leave me. I knew from her face that she wasn't lying.

So what did I do? "Enforced recovery," I suppose, might be the best term for what I then attempted, but, like most things, nothing can come of any attempt that has no will-power behind it and it proved impossible for me to excise the bulimia entirely. Mostly, this is because I had no desire to. I live with my girlfriend now. The rhythm I've settled into is one in which I eat carefully in the evenings when she's home, and it's usually something very different to what she's eating. It is a meal worthy of my anorexic days because I know I'll be unable to purge it and I will never try to. I have no desire to have her leave me because of bulimia, which is, at least, one step further than many more unfortunate bulimics have managed to go. So, having worked out, via the medium of some very uncomfortable erroneous tries, that purging while she's with me and hoping she won't notice is foolhardy at best, potentially life-shattering at worst, I have stopped doing it entirely. I love my girl-friend. I love her a lot.

The fact remains, however, that there are other things I love. I love eating high calorie foods with no sense of guilt, something I can only do if I know that the food will be evacuated from my body in all its gooey, sticky, lubricated glory, as soon as I've eaten as much as my stomach can hold. I love being slim and feeling sexy, as much for my girlfriend as for myself. The combination of these two things over-rides my distaste for withheld truths and as a consequence I tend to binge and purge at least once a day during term time, while my girlfriend, who has now graduated, is at work and I am engaged in the necessary work on my degree. It is, for me, the best compromise I can currently achieve. I do sometimes wish that my girlfriend could have been like my ex-girlfriend, or that my ex-girlfriend and I could have felt the same way about each other that my current girlfriend and I do, but in my heart I'm glad that neither of these eventualities came to pass. Although I'm not completely ready to recover from bulimia just yet, I have no desire to be 45 and still obsessed with food. And I know that if I had been in a relationship with another bulimic, there would never have been any incentive to stop. We would have gone on until our teeth had rotted and our hearts were as shrunken and frail as our bodies. In short, we would have destroyed each other.

Today, my girlfriend knows I have issues with food and is as supportive as could be expected from somebody who has never had any such difficulties herself. After several long and tearful conversations on the subject, we've come to the understanding that there are certain things that are "unsafe" for me and which I categorically will not eat, ever. She never tries to make me eat anything in the evenings. I always make, or if we're eating out then I choose, my own food. She knows she can eat whatever she likes and that I'll be quite happy to cook it for her, but that, if she wants me to recover, she mustn't expect me to eat the same foods. As for my ex-girlfriend, we're still best friends and the last time we met up we did indeed strike out on a rampage of the LBM, but her views on ultimate recovery goals are much the same as mine. Neither of us wants to be a middle-aged, lonely bulimic and we're both agreed that other things are much more important. In the best of fantasy worlds, we'd like to be fairly comfortable around food most of the time, with the means and capacity to binge as an indulgence perhaps once or twice a week. Really, we both know anyone who still thinks of purging as an option, in any sense, will never quite be comfortable around food. We're also very aware it's unlikely that anyone who's been as deeply entrenched in eating disorders as we have will ever think of food in a normal way again. But we're both far better than we were. We're taking it step by step. We will recover. Some day, we'll want to recover entirely and when we want it, we'll be able to do it.

Today is not that day, but I'm 99 percent sure, now, that it'll come.

19

Diets Don't Work, Bulimia Does

I returned to the dinner table in time to hear my mother groan, "I'm so full already," as she looked at all the delicious dishes still waiting to be devoured. "Amateur," I quipped playfully, having just finished throwing up the main course in the bathroom to make room in my stomach for dessert. I could hear a combination of envy and admiration in her voice as she laughed and gave some trite line in reply that I can no longer recall. For a moment I felt a surge of self-satisfied smugness. I was good at the game nearly every woman in the western world plays at some time in her life, only to fail in the end. Never mind that I was only good because I cheated.

For as long as I remember, my mother has always been dieting, losing and gaining the same ten pounds over and over again. So based on what I saw her put herself through, I was convinced in my teens of the fact that diets do not work; something that has since been confirmed by countless studies, even those sponsored by companies peddling miracle weight loss methods. Much like my mother, well over 90 percent of dieters end up gaining back the weight they lost and often more.

Beyond that early flash of enlightenment though, I did not exactly break any other molds of social conditioning. I was chubby and detested my body like everything and everyone around me was suggesting I should, until I reached my early twenties and found that while diets do not work, obsession and eating disorders do. At what cost it never even occurred to me to ask myself. What could be more important than procuring the modern holy grail of thinness?

So I put myself and my body through restriction and compulsive exercise for a few years, my weight fluctuating between the diagnoses for anorexia and eating disorder not otherwise specified. I was perversely proud to be considered anorexic. Not because anorexia itself was the goal, it merely signified I had achieved unquestionable thinness. It would still be a few years until the likes of extremely thin starlets became the tabloid-lauded stick figure darlings of our celebrity-obsessed world, but a certain actress was already on my television screen and making headlines in the media for her frail looking figure. There was a collective voice of envy and admiration shining through the expressions of concern for her health and well-being. I could not trust what the mirror or the scales told me about my body, but the judgment of others, especially medical professionals, provided me with all the validation I needed. Being compared to the media certified anorexics such as these emaciated looking celebrities meant I was successful.

Of course, like my mother discovered through her dieting, the body can only take so much neglect and abuse before it fights back. After two days of severe restriction, on the third I'd be gorging myself on, well, anything at all I could find in my fridge and cupboards. On the fourth, I'd take a trip to the grocery store and gorge some more. On the fifth… It should go without saying that this soon started to sabotage my hard won status of being an anorexic and thus certifiably thin. That is when I learned to cheat.

I do not consider myself bulimic. Throwing up is a safety valve for me. I eat my cake and stay thin. I eat my pizza and my ice cream and lose weight. Then I eat some more cake, pizza, ice cream, cookies, chocolate, and go make myself throw up. After that, I feel drowsy, so I lie down and try to take a nap, while worrying whether I got up everything I ate and whether it will make me gain significant weight if I did not. Scared of the potential weight gain, I decide to stop the shenanigans and restrict again. I usually manage to do this for a few days, but then the food fantasies become overwhelmingly strong again and I find myself heading straight towards the candy aisle… I guess I might be bulimic after all.

My obsession is not about control or denying myself what I do not think I deserve. It is not about punishing myself. It is about perfectionism, about achievement. Sometimes it is about attention. It is about wanting to be the thinnest person, no, woman in the room. Because the thinnest, in my thinking (but definitely not only mine), equals the best. Everyone wants to lose weight, to know how you became thin or how you stay that way, to congratulate you, to gush over the new tiny you. They ask you to share your secrets. They envy you for your strength. It feels powerful to be in the possession of something that so many want, yet so few have.

I recognize these reasons as quite shallow and the competition as petty and pointless, even harmful, not only to myself but to other women as well. Yet I (choose to) engage in this behavior anyway. I must be either immoral or sick. I confess I do not know which I am, or which I'd rather be...

"Why is being thin so important to you?" my psychiatrist asked during a recent meeting. The question sounds so simple, yet I did not know how to answer it. Why is being thin so important to me that I am willing to go to such torturous lengths to achieve it? Why is it more important than being healthy and feeling good? Why would I rather be successful at being thin than anything else?

Why is being thin so important to me, I asked myself later the same day when bent over the bath tub, fingers jabbing the back of my throat, to rid my body of my dinner, of its nutrition and energy. Am I that vain? At what point does vanity stop being shallow and cross over to sick?

Why is being thin so important to us? Not just those of us who fit the diagnostic criteria for eating disorders, but to almost every other woman as well. The line between "eating disordered" and "normal" has become increasingly blurred. It is "normal" for women to worry about and watch their weight, it is "normal" to go on restrictive diets that resemble an eating disordered person's daily routine. Looking around me, that is what I see women do. I see it on television and on billboards; I read about it in magazines and on the internet; I hear it from friends, colleagues, relatives. In this light my obsession seems nothing special. I just take it that little bit further. I am just a little bit more dedicated.

Why is being thin so important to me? I do not love my mother any more or any less, whether she weighs 150 or

100 pounds. She would not love me less if I weighed 150 instead of 100 pounds. I do not care about the weight of my friends or co-workers and I hope they do not care about mine either. Does this mean the opinions of strangers, most of whom I have never met and never will, are so important to me?

At this point in the discussion, the finger is often pointed at the media for encouraging this type of thin-or-nothing thinking. And the media make it easy to do so, with the unrelenting parade of thin and thinner stars on the covers of newspapers and magazines and the constant shaming of any unfortunate (usually female) celebrity who happens to have gained weight or flashed a bit of cellulite on the beach.

I do not want to blame the media or portray myself as the victim here. We are the ones who accept the message that is passed to us. We are the ones taking the cues from our mothers and passing them on to our daughters. This is not to say we should blame ourselves, but that ultimately we are the only ones who can stop this cycle being perpetuated. When the whole society is eating disordered in its outlook, the scope of the problem has become too wide for us to rely on doctors alone for a solution.

No, I do not know how to stop it. If I did, I would not be here writing this. I would be far away living happily ever after.

Further Reading

Duker, M. and Slade, R. (1988) *Anorexia Nervosa and Bulimia: How to Help*. Philadelphia: Open University Press.

This book provides myriad invaluable, productive and important information on the recovery from an eating disorder based on many years of practice with anorexic and bulimic patients. Introduced with and based on their whirlpool theory to the understanding of eating disorders, very useful guidance is included for those wanting to help individuals with bulimia or anorexia so as not to trigger and increase the intensity of the eating disordered behaviors.

Fairburn, C. G. (1995) *Overcoming Binge Eating*. New York: Guilford Press.

Details a "six steps" self-help program ensuring a steady and easy-to-follow progression through each stage of recovery. Each stage is explained and illustrated in a simple and straightforward manner, complete with useful advice, tables, checklists and questions, as well as advice on when to progress to the next step of the program. There is also a section on alternative options to do instead of engaging in eating disordered behaviors.

Gomez, J. (1995) *How to Cope with Bulimia*. London: Sheldon Press.

Provides a description of bulimia, the signs and symptoms, the health risks associated with it, personal and family issues, issues with sex and relationships, coping with the disorder as a mother, guidance on recovering with the disorder and a chapter to find out if you are at risk of developing the disorder and the preventative measure to be taken. The book includes a quiz and weight tables.

Hornbacher, M. (1998) *Wasted*. London: HarperCollins.

A memoir written by Marya Hornbacher at the age of 23, who developed bulimia aged 9 and anorexia aged 15. *Wasted* is a brutally honest and harrowing account of bulimia and anorexia. Hornbacher has a talent for drawing the reader into her world; a gift for setting out the scene of the dark, murky violence of living with, and almost dying of, an eating disorder. She details the agony of the irreversible internal and external damage developed through her years of abusing her body. The book ends with Hornbacher on the road to recovery, accurately painted as an incredibly difficult and painful journey, suggesting she will have many relapses in the future as she continually struggles to recover.

Maine, M. (1991) *Father Hunger: Fathers, Daughters & Food.* Carlsbad, CA: Gürze Books.

Father Hunger explores the father–daughter relationship and its role in the daughter's attitude to food. The book promotes the idea of male influence on eating disorders and the father–daughter conflicts and dilemmas of an emotional absent father causing the daughter to feel emotional emptiness and turn to food as a substitute for the father's love or to use food as a mask. Maine offers practical solutions for these problems. The book is divided into three parts consisting of the origins and experience of, as well as the solutions to, father hunger.

Reindl, S. M. (2001) *Sensing the Self.* Cambridge, MA: Harvard University Press.

Provides a depiction of the journey of recovery from bulimia. Reindl believes an important aspect of recovery is looking inside and addressing the issues of shame and rediscovering feelings and emotions that were previously repressed and pushed aside. *Sensing the Self* includes research, Reindl's subjective experience in a clinical setting and guidance on the effective continuation of recovering and not falling back into the security of the disorder.

Schmidt, U. and Treasure, J. (1993) *Getting Better Bit(e) by Bit(e)*. Hove: Psychology Press.

Originally written for the use of patients of the Maudsley Hospital, it provides a plethora of tools and guidance to begin recovery from bulimia or binge eating. The book is filled with strategies to avoid the pitfalls many sufferers face in recovery and the advice to bounce back on the right path. There are also many short accounts interspersed throughout the book from sufferers who have experienced the pitfalls of recovery. It includes a test to see if you have the symptoms of bulimia and also the severity of your symptoms. This book tackles not only dieting and binging and purging, but also issues of body image, self-esteem, guilt, exercising, relapsing and sexual abuse, among other issues.

Shelley, R. (1997) *Anorexics on Anorexia*. London: Jessica Kingsley Publishers.

Shelley has edited a compilation of 19 stories written by sufferers of anorexia nervosa in all stages of the disorder or on the path to recovery. The stories reflect the wide range of individuals suffering from the disorder, their similarities as well as their unique struggles with the disorder. *Anorexics on Anorexia* provides hope to those suffering with anorexia. It gives an in-depth portrayal of the internal conflicts of coping with anorexia, illustrating the "distressing and bleak" nature of the disorder. Among the many themes that are covered in the stories are anger, addiction, childhood anorexia and having an alcoholic parent.

Anorexics on Anorexia

Edited by Rosemary Shelley

Paperback, ISBN 978 1 85302 471 9, 172 pages

'…The book will give insights to those caring for people with anorexia and support for others with the illness.'

— Eating Disorders Association.

'Its strength lies in communicating the meaning or the value of anorexia to the person who has it. This is an aspect of the condition that others find hard to grasp. This book is also valuable in that it allows people with anorexia to 'have a voice', something which has clearly been denied to many of them in their accounts of their experiences of treatment.'

— Nursing Times

'The stories told are emotive and very personal, and offer insight into how some sufferers have experienced life and the interventions of the professionals. The book would undoubtedly be useful for the individual who is suffering alone and seeking shared experiences [and] also a useful read for professionals new to the field as an insight into how some people with eating disorders might think and feel.'

— Clinical Child Psychology and Psychiatry

'Anorexia is not an illness experienced just by teenage girls and the contributors to this book reflect that. They represent a cross-section of sufferers from pre-adolescence to middle age and beyond. There are accounts from both males and females. They speak of different treatment methods, some effective, others highly ineffective and even damaging. The different issues, problems, worries and traumas that triggered the onset of their eating problems are also analysed in detail… More importantly, however, this book has been written for those suffering from the illness. Anorexia is a highly complex problem that is often difficult to understand especially for those going through it. This book aims to unravel some of that confusion and help sufferers to understand themselves and their behaviour more fully.'

— From the Introduction

Recovering sufferers of Anorexia Nervosa describe in their own words their personal experiences of this illness, providing not only support for fellow sufferers but also invaluable insights for the families of sufferers and for carers and professionals. In each case the contributors describe:

- the progression of their illness
- the effect on their families
- the treatment they received and its effectiveness
- their perceived reasons for developing the illness
- where they are now.

Beating Eating Disorders Step by Step
A Self-Help Guide for Recovery

Anna Paterson

Paperback, ISBN 978 1 84310 340 0, 224 pages

People living with eating disorders find it hard to take the step of choosing recovery, often because the disorder has developed as a way of 'coping' with problems or stresses in the their life. This book outlines new and positive ways of dealing with eating disorders for people living with eating disorders and their families.

A practical workbook written by someone who has lived with eating disorder, it provides advice and strategies to aid understanding and to help the reader to gain control of their illness. Anna Paterson leads the reader through easy-to-use therapeutic exercises, such as describing the pros and cons of an illness, writing a farewell letter to it, and using role-reversal scenarios to get a new perspective on their attitude to eating. She emphasizes the importance of taking things at your own pace and in the final section of the book provides a set of diet plans specifically designed for anorexics, bulimics and compulsive overeaters.

This book will be valued by people living with eating disorders and their families, and also the psychologists and psychotherapists, counsellors, health professionals and social workers who work with them.

Anna Paterson lived for 14 years with chronic anorexia. Since her recovery she has published a number of books on eating disorders, including *Running on Empty*, winner of the Times NASEN 2002 Children's Book Award, and *Diet of Despair*, which was given a special commendation in the Times NASEN 2002 Non-Fiction category. She participated in a 2001 BBC documentary entitled 'Quietly Dying' and has featured in *B* Magazine, the *Daily Express*, the *Independent*, the *Times Educational Supplement*, *Women's Own* and *You* magazine. She is a frequent speaker on eating disorders and volunteers as an eating disorders helpline operator. Anna lives in London.

Inside Anorexia
The Experiences of Girls and their Families

Christine Halse, Anne Hone, and Desiree Boughtwood

Paperback, ISBN 978 1 84310 597 8, 208 pages

Inside Anorexia provides valuable insight into the experiences and challenges faced by teenage girls with anorexia and their families.

The authors use the stories of individuals and their families as a starting point for understanding the issues associated with anorexia including: physical effects, the effect on siblings and parents, related psychiatric problems, causes and treatment. Useful fact boxes in each story provide an overview of current knowledge from a variety of disciplines as well as new findings from the authors' own research into anorexia nervosa.

Inside Anorexia is an accessible resource for anyone who wants a better understanding of anorexia nervosa. It will be an informative guide for health professionals as well as for people with anorexia and their families.

Dr Christine Halse is an Associate Professor in Education and Chief Investigator of the multi-disciplinary, multi-method Australian Research Council project, *Multiple Perspectives of Eating Disorders in Girls,* at the University of Western Sydney, Australia. Her research and publications on anorexia nervosa have addressed biographical, clinical and ethical issues.

Dr Anne Honey is Senior Researcher with the *Multiple Perspectives of Eating Disorders in Girls* project at the University of Western Sydney and has a background in mental health research and occupational therapy.

Dr Desiree Boughtwood is a counselor. Her doctorate, titled *Anorexia Nervosa in the Clinic,* examined teenage girls' experiences of hospitalization for anorexic nervosa.

Drawing from Within
Using Art to Treat Eating Disorders

Lisa D. Hinz

Paperback, ISBN 978 1 84310 822 1, 192 pages

'I recommend this book to anyone who is interested in developments in person-centred therapy or in thinking about the use of art as a therapeutic tool; it is clearly structured and well-organised and clearly a valuable contribution to the field of psychological therapy and training.'
— *Routledge, Taylor and Francis Group*

'The book is fantastic — it is well written, accurate and well backed up with current research findings and references. There are some wonderful ideas within the book and each is presented in such a practical way that you find they immediately bring to mind clients for whom they might be helpful.'
— *Lifeline, Anorexia and Bulimia Care Spring 2007*

Drawing from Within is an introductory guide for those wanting to explore the use of art with clients with eating disorders. Art therapy is a particularly effective therapeutic intervention for this group, as it allows them to express uncomfortable thoughts and feelings through artistic media rather than having to explain them verbally.

Lisa D. Hinz outlines the areas around which the therapist can design effective treatment programmes, covering family influences, body image, self-acceptance, problem solving and spirituality. Each area is discussed in a separate chapter and is accompanied by suggestions for exercises, with advice on materials to use and how to implement them. Case examples show how a therapy programme can be tailored to the individual client and photographs of client artwork illustrate the text throughout.

Practical and accessible to practitioners at all levels of experience, this book gives new hope to therapists and other mental health professionals who want to explore the potential of using art with clients with eating disorders.

Lisa D. Hinz is a clinical psychologist and a registered art therapist. She received a PhD in psychology from Louisiana State University and a post-doctoral certificate in art therapy from the University of Louisville. She currently lectures at the Centre for Health at St. Helena Hospital, CA, and is also an adjunct professor in art therapy at Saint Mary-of-the-Woods College. Dr Hinz has been helping people with eating disorders for more than 20 years.

In and Out of Anorexia
The Story of the Client, the Therapist and the Process of Recovery

Tammie Ronen and Ayelet

Paperback, ISBN 978 1 85302 990 5, 288 pages

'A detailed and compelling account of a young woman's struggle with anorexia nervosa. Certainly, the professional will learn from these insights, perhaps understanding better their patients' experiences and language. They are likely to benefit, too, from thinking about Ronen's patient-centred, individualised and creative approach'

– Young Minds

'One of the striking things about this story is Tammie's ability to speak her client's language. Through adapting a variety of therapeutic techniques into Ayelet's language of metaphors, imagery and art, Tammie not only enhanced the effectiveness of these techniques but established a therapeutic alliance based on collaboration and openness.'

– British Journal of Clinical Psychology

Ayelet spent six years of her adolescence in and out of hospital, having been diagnosed as suffering from a severe anorexia disorder. She is now a special needs teacher. In the first part of this book Ayelet describes her personal experiences of the illness, the repeated hospitalisations and her ultimate recovery, illustrated with examples of her drawing and writing from when she was ill.

Tammie Ronen, her therapist, outlines the step-by-step progress of the therapy from the professional angle, describing in detail the decision-making and treatment considerations specific to Ayelet's life and context. She also includes comprehensive overviews of contemporary research into anorexia and of cognitive constructivist methods. The book is a rich source of inspiration and guidance for therapists and other professionals, as well as for people with eating disorders and their families.

Tammie Ronen is a senior lecturer and head of the counselling programme in child clinical studies at the Bob Shapell School of Social Work at Tel Aviv University; she also heads the university research centre for child treatment and empowerment. She is president of the Israeli Association for Behaviour and Cognitive Therapy. She is an experienced supervisor and therapist. She has published and lectured widely around the world and is the author of *Cognitive Developmental Therapy with Children*. **Ayelet** is a special education teacher.

A Systemic Treatment of Bulimia Nervosa
Women in Transition

Carole Kayrooz
Foreword by a service user

Paperback, ISBN 978 1 85302 918 9, 176 pages

'In contrast to the treatment of anorexia nervosa, not much has been written about systemic approaches to bulimia nervosa, and this book is a very good starting point... There is a wealth of clinical material here which illustrates the approach through three detailed and evocative case studies. I would recommend this book to any practitioner on the field of eating disorders.'
– Child and Adolescent Mental Health

'The strength of this book is that it is accessible, easy to read, very practical and has a strong practice focus. It provides some excellent ideas for intervention with people with eating disorders, many of which would be transferred to other areas of practice and the case studies bring the application of theory, technique and task setting to life. The author is clearly passionate about her subject and this is often reflected in vivid and evocative prose.

This book will certainly be of interest to anyone working in the field of eating disorders and represents a useful addition to the literature in this area.'
– British Journal of Social Work

Written in an accessible and jargon-free way, this original approach to working with women who have bulimia nervosa is based on research showing that bulimia nervosa involves interpersonal, social and societal factors as well as the cognitive, developmental and behavioural aspects that have been the focus of much professional intervention to date. Carole Kayrooz shows how people seeking to understand and emotionally support women with this complex problem need to be able to work with all these dimensions. Her book is one of the first to interpret the disorder within a systems framework and to present a detailed systemic model for its treatment. By applying systems theory to the problem, the author highlights its contextual nature.

The practical application of this multi-dimensional, systems-based understanding to treatment practice is demonstrated through three in-depth case studies. This book is essential reading for psychologists, counsellors, therapists, social workers, and health professionals working with this group, as well as for people suffering from bulimia nervosa and their families.

Carole Kayrooz is an academic and psychologist at the University of Canberra.